Taunton's
BUILD LIKE A PRO®
EXPERT ADVICE FROM START TO FINISH

Building
Outdoor
Structures

Taunton's

BUILD LIKE A PRO®
EXPERT ADVICE FROM START TO FINISH

Building Outdoor Structures

Scott McBride

The Taunton Press

The Taunton Press
Inspiration for hands-on living®

The Taunton Press, Inc., 63 South Main Street, P.O. Box 5506, Newtown, CT 06470-5506
e-mail: tp@taunton.com

EDITOR: Jennifer Renjilian Morris
COVER DESIGN: Lori Wendin and Kimberly Adis
INTERIOR DESIGN: Kimberly Adis
LAYOUT: Cathy Cassidy
COVER PHOTOGRAPHERS: Front cover, clockwise from top left: © Jerry Pavia Photography, Inc.; Christopher Ermides, © The Taunton Press, Inc.; Scott McBride; Back cover, clockwise from left: © Brian Vanden Brink; Scott McBride; Scott McBride
PHOTOGRAPHERS: All photographs by Scott McBride, except the following: p. 4: Andrew Kline; pp. 6, 8 top right, 9 top and bottom: Sandor Nagyszalanczy, © The Taunton Press, Inc.; p. 26: Janet Delaney; pp. 46, 146 left: davidduncanlivingston.com; p. 60-61: Todd Meier, © The Taunton Press, Inc.; p. 61 top: © Tim Street-Porter; p. 61 right: © Erik Kvalsvik; pp. 61 bottom, 75 top, 108 middle and bottom, 124–125 spread, 125 bottom, 153: © Lee Anne White; p. 66: Peter Kreyling; p. 74 top: Brian Pontolilo, © The Taunton Press, Inc., bottom courtesy Allan Block; pp. 74-75, 109 top: Virginia Small, © The Taunton Press, Inc.; p. 88 top: Marc Vassallo, © The Taunton Press, Inc.; bottom © Saxon Holt/Photo Botanic; p. 89 top: Lee Anne White, © The Taunton Press, Inc.; bottom © judywhite/GardenPhotos.com; pp. 108-109, 150: © Brian Vanden Brink; p. 124 top & left: Boyd Hagen, © The Taunton Press, Inc.; p. 125 top: © J. Paul Moore; p. 146 right: Delilah Smittle, © The Taunton Press, Inc.; p. 147 top right: © Michael Gertley, bottom © Allan Mandell; pp. 156 top, 157 top left & right, 157 middle, 158 right & bottom, 159 top, 160 top middle, 161 bottom, 162–165: Frank Schmidt; p. 156 bottom, 157 bottom, 158 top, 159 bottom, 160 top left & right, 160 bottom, p. 161 left & right: Amy Wysocki; p. 166: top: © Alan & Linda Detrick, bottom Jennifer Brown, © The Taunton Press, Inc.; p. 167 left: © www.kenricephoto.com; right © Mark Turner; p. 182: Photo courtesy Trex
ILLUSTRATOR: Michael Gellatly

Library of Congress Cataloging-in-Publication Data
McBride, Scott.
  Building outdoor structures / Scott McBride.
      p. cm.
  Includes index.
  ISBN 978-1-56158-939-5
  1. Garden structures--Design and construction. I. Title.
TH4961.M376 2007
690--dc22
                          2007005186

Printed in China
10 9 8 7 6 5 4 3 2 1

The following manufacturers/names appearing in *Building Outdoor Structures* are trademarks: Masonite®, Osmose®, Parallam Trus Joist®, Photoshop™, Redi-Mix®, Speed® square, Titebond III®, Trex®, WD-40®, Wolmanized®

Working wood is inherently dangerous. Using hand or power tools improperly or ignoring safety practices can lead to permanent injury or even death. Don't try to perform operations you learn about here (or elsewhere) unless you're certain they are safe for you. If something about an operation doesn't feel right, don't do it. Look for another way. We want you to enjoy the craft, so please keep safety foremost in your mind whenever you're in the shop.

For Nancy

ACKNOWLEDGMENTS

First I would like to thank my old pal Kevin Ireton for nominating me to write this book. Over the years he has done as much as anyone to turn a ranting carpenter into a technical journalist. Other contributors to that process were Mark Feirer, John Lively, and many others.

I have been shepherded through my first book by three expert ladies. Helen Albert helped me hammer out a vision for the book and kept faith in me despite several false starts. Thanks, Helen. Cherilyn DeVries kept the effort chugging along and held my hand through several bouts of computer hysteria. The lion's share of the job went to Jennifer Renjilian Morris. Working on a skin-tight schedule, she managed to rope in my unruly manuscript with care and sensitivity. I wish to thank Holly Pendleton, Roe Osborn, and Rita Meyers for coaching me on computers, and Steve Dudley for his advice on photo equipment. I would like to thank *someone* for telling me how to take good pictures, but I have finally concluded that nobody can do that except the

merciless camera. Chuck Miller came the closest when I begged him for a few morsels of photo wisdom. "You'll do fine, kid," he said. "You've got the eye."

Thanks to my brother in faith John A. Jenkins for his recommendations on paths—the garden variety as well as the spiritual kind. Special thanks to master builders Peter Kreyling and Kevin Weisgerber for sharing their knowledge of retaining walls. Thanks also to landscape designers Brendan Foster and Elizabeth Martin for their expertise on garden matters.

I'm indebted to my photo models Kevin, Nan, Ryan, and Terry for their patience ("Just hold that oak beam up for *one more minute*. . .") and to the many people who let a complete stranger walk into their yards to take pictures.

Thanks to my parents Al and Barbara McBride, who taught me to love beautiful books as well as beautiful homes. Finally, a special word of appreciation to my high school shop teacher, Mr. Joe Tibbs, wherever you are. Your encouragement meant so much.

CONTENTS

INTRODUCTION

There's a little bit of wood-worker in every gardener, starting with the first twig used to skewer a seed packet. I began building wooden structures for our family garden 20 years ago. I didn't know much about horticulture or carpentry, but my ignorance was superseded by my enthusiasm. Consequently, I made my share of mistakes. I built retaining walls with untreated barn timbers that rotted after a season. To make arches, I joined wooden segments with plywood splines; the plywood speedily delaminated. The 2×4 borders around our vegetable bed heaved because of inadequate drainage, and our impatiens languished in too-shallow planters I built. One day the building inspector even showed up to inform me that the 400 ft. of scrolled picket fence I had just built around our property was a foot too high.

The craftsman in me was chagrined by these failures, but the knowing farmer inside just shrugged. After all, disappointment is a perennial visitor to any adventurous gardener, who knows that this year's disaster lays the foundation for next year's bumper crop.

Success in my endeavors often was as unexpected as my failures—the grapevine that covered the arbor I built in just two years, the trellis that cast eerie shadows by night when a lantern was placed inside. Encouraged by the victories, I continued to adorn our little Eden. Eventually the place began to teeter dangerously on the brink of looking like a miniature theme park, plunked down mysteriously on a suburban side street.

Carpentry eventually became my career, whereas gardening remained a hobby. Though my enjoyment of woodworking has evolved as my skills and tools have grown, I have rarely again experienced the thrill of seeing those early garden structures pop up in the landscape. Unencumbered by the finicky tolerances of indoor carpentry, and without a client to please, I was free to conjure up a design and execute it in a single Saturday. Wood, with its moderate cost and yielding nature, was the perfect material for such impulsive escapades. More often than not, the results were satisfying. In the season that followed, I watched with pleasure as my creations posed against the shifting backdrops of summer verdure, autumn color, and winter white.

Building Outdoor Structures starts at the beginning of the building process with instructions for planning and everything you need to know before you build. You'll learn how to choose tools that are right for the job and materials that will endure. Once you know the basics, you'll learn the nuts and bolts of building outdoor structures, from foundations and framing to finishes.

But the heart of the book deals with the structures themselves, from simple borders to more involved projects like arbors and trellises. You'll find general building guidelines for each type of structure, as well as detailed step-by-step instructions and photos illustrating how to build a basic example of each structure.

This book includes general construction information, accompanied by step-by-step photos to make the instructions easier to follow. There are also Pro Tips, Trade Secrets, and What Can Go Wrong sidebars so you

get even more information. To show you some of the many ways you might incorporate these projects into your home or your clients' homes, we've created a Design Options spread at the end of each project chapter. There you'll find different looks that go beyond the construction basics of the text and show you what else is possible.

It is my hope that *Building Outdoor Structures* will spare you some of my painful mistakes and point the way to garden structures that embody those much-sought-after virtues of good building: firmness, commodity, and delight.

4

TOOLS AND MATERIALS

Learning to build means entering into an extended dialogue with your materials and tools. By trial and error, they will tell you what you can and cannot do. Nail a board too close to the end and it will split. But drilling a quick pilot hole with a cordless drill beforehand solves the problem.

Other lessons don't show up until after the job is done. For instance, wood that hasn't been seasoned properly may look great when you pack up your tools, but in a few weeks your perfect joints will open up as a result of shrinkage. Similarly, using plain ungalvanized fasteners with pressure-treated lumber will mean doing the job over again in just a few years when the fasteners corrode.

Although most of these lessons aren't too painful, there are some you'll want to avoid at all costs. Hopefully the safety pointers in this chapter will keep you from learning the hard way. ▶ ▶ ▶

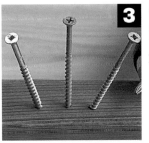

Tools

Some basic hand tools and power tools will be enough to do most of the projects in this book. Sometimes, you can make life easier for yourself if you use a specialty tool, but there are always ways to use the basics. Here, you'll see what tools and what extras you need for outdoor projects.

Your basic tool rig

A good tool pouch keeps your most-used hand tools within easy reach. Those tools are a hammer, measuring tape, speed square, nail puller, and chalkline.

A hammer with a straight claw (also called a rip claw) is better for outdoor carpentry than a curved-claw hammer because the straight claw doubles as a digging tool. Wood handles are short-lived, but fiberglass handles are durable, and they don't transmit vibration as much as all-steel handles.

A 25-ft. auto-rewind tape will handle most of your measuring needs, although a 100-ft. manual-rewind tape also comes in handy for big projects like fences. Similarly, a lightweight triangular speed square covers most layout work and fits neatly in a tool pouch, but occasionally you'll need a framing square for bigger jobs.

A nail puller, also called a "cat's paw," can dig under the head of a fully driven nail and then lever out the nail. If the nail is a large one, however, it's easier to start the job with a nail puller and then switch to a longer type of bar for more leverage.

A chalkline lets you snap a perfectly straight line anywhere. A line without chalk is called a dry-line; it's useful for aligning fence posts and such.

Handsaw

Handsaws fall into two broad categories—crosscut and rip. As the name implies, crosscut saws cut across the grain of a board. To "rip" a board, on the other hand, means to cut a board along the grain, sort of like ripping a rag in half along the weave of the cloth. The difference between crosscut and rip saws lies in the teeth; crosscut teeth are shaped like tiny knives that sever wood fibers, whereas rip teeth are shaped like tiny chisels that scoop out "noodles" of wood along the grain.

The number of teeth on a saw determines the speed and smoothness of cut. A saw that has many small teeth will cut slowly but leaves a fine finish, whereas a saw with fewer but larger teeth

Handsaws come in different lengths and tooth patterns. For rough garden carpentry a saw with medium to large teeth works well.

Cutting with a Handsaw

THE TRICK TO ACHIEVING A SQUARE EDGE with a handsaw is to get the saw started correctly. Position yourself so that you can see both the mark on the face of the workpiece and the mark on the edge. Move your head until these two marks appear as a straight line.

Now bring the blade of your handsaw up to the mark (see the drawing at right). Rotate the blade until its sides disappear and the top edge of the blade is all you see. Then adjust the saw sideways until it aligns with the combined face mark/edge mark on the work. Maintain a relaxed grip on the saw, with your forearm in line with the direction of the cut.

When starting the cut, place the thumb of your free hand against the blade to steady it (see the photo at left). Now draw the blade back toward you slowly. (If you try to push the blade at this point, it may skip around and cut your thumb!) A few gentle pull strokes will start a groove, or kerf, for the saw to ride in. Once a groove is established, you can begin sawing. Use long, easy strokes, and concentrate on keeping the blade, the face mark, and the edge mark all lined up.

Use your thumb to guide the saw when starting the cut. A few gentle pull strokes will establish a kerf for the blade to ride in.

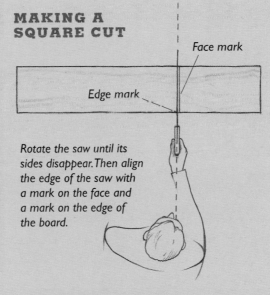

MAKING A SQUARE CUT

Face mark

Edge mark

Rotate the saw until its sides disappear. Then align the edge of the saw with a mark on the face and a mark on the edge of the board.

will cut fast and leave a coarse finish. Number of teeth is specified in teeth-per-inch, or TPI. For garden projects, a medium- to coarse-cutting saw, such as an 8 TPI crosscut, works well. Finer-toothed saws are for interior trim jobs.

In recent years Japanese-style handsaws have gained wide acceptance in the West. These cut on the pull-stroke rather than the push-stroke, as is the case with Western-style handsaws.

Chisels and planes

Chisels are used for chopping out waste wood and shaving flat surfaces. They can be pushed by hand (a technique called paring) or driven with a hammer or mallet. Plastic chisel handles can withstand the blows of a hammer, but wood-handled chisels should be beaten with a mallet to avoid damage.

A block plane is used to shave the edge of a board.

Cordless drills can drive screws as well as make holes. This model has an adjustable clutch that regulates turning power so you won't strip the heads on small, delicate screws.

WHAT CAN GO WRONG

When planing the edge of a board you may have trouble keeping the edge square (perpendicular) to the face. This happens when a plane iron sticks out more on one side than the other. Gauge the setting by gently feeling the projection of the iron beyond the bottom of the plane, first on one side, then the other. To adjust, tap the side of the plane iron, or use the adjusting lever, depending on the type of plane you have.

Planes are essentially chisels held in a body that controls their cutting depth. The first plane bodies were wood, but longer-wearing iron bodies were developed in the 19th century. Iron planes were also easier to adjust.

The handiest plane for carpentry work is the block plane. It's a small plane designed to be used with one hand. To plane the edge of a board, plant one end of the board against something solid and push the plane in the direction of the grain (see the photo above left). If the plane iron, or blade, is sharp, one long, curled shaving will pirouette out of the tool. Experiment with the depth-of-cut adjusting screw to find the most effective setting.

To plane the face of a board, push the plane across the grain, producing thin wafers. The resulting surface will be rough but even—it can be sanded smooth. Planing the face of a board with the grain usually tears and digs into the surface.

Cordless drills

Cordless drills are ideal for landscape carpentry, where electricity is often beyond reach. Good cordless drills aren't cheap, but no other power

tool will get more use around your home and garden.

Every few years, a new generation of cordless drills arrives that is more powerful and longer-running than the last—36 volts is the top dog at present. You'll appreciate the extra power and running time of 18-volt to 36-volt models if you're boring large-diameter holes or driving long screws, but for most jobs a 12-volt drill is adequate. Lower-voltage models are lighter and less expensive.

Most cordless drills have an adjustable clutch to regulate the tool's torque (twisting power). If screw heads are snapping off as they're being tightened, reduce the clutch setting. If a drill bogs down or a screw won't drive, increase the setting for more "oomph."

In addition to the clutch setting, torque is also controlled by speed range. Most drills have a high-speed/low-torque setting and a low-speed/high-torque setting. (Actual speed varies within these ranges according to trigger pressure.) Use the high-speed range for drilling small holes, and the low-speed range for drilling large-diameter holes and for driving screws.

Jigsaws

Compared to a circular saw, a jigsaw (or saber saw) is versatile and safe. Its narrow blade cuts curves easily, and because it produces less friction, kickback is virtually eliminated. On the down-side, a jigsaw cuts slower than a circular saw and doesn't produce as straight a cut.

The difference in performance between homeowner and professional models is especially noticeable in the jigsaw family. Professional models have an elliptical blade motion that cuts much more efficiently than the straight up-and-down motion of homeowner types. Professional jigsaws also have a guide bearing that supports the blade, giving better control. The projects illustrated in this book can be tackled with a homeowner-type jigsaw, but the job will take longer. Try out different models, and buy the best you can afford.

For landscape carpentry, a coarse-toothed blade is usually all you'll need. If you desire a smooth edge, switch to a fine-toothed blade or sand the edges.

Jigsaws are great for cutting curves like those found on fancy pickets and arches. They also make straight cuts.

Circular saw

A portable circular saw takes much of the exertion out of carpentry—it can cut through a 2×4 in about two seconds. But this tool is also dangerous because it can cut through a hand or finger just as easily. Because there's no way to react quickly enough to avert an accident, it's essential that the tool be used safely at all times.

Safety A circular saw is among the noisiest and dustiest of all power tools, so wear ear and eye protection when using one. You'll also need to protect against kickback, one of the primary hazards of using a circular saw. Kickback usu-

Portable circular saws make straight cuts quickly. A cordless model (such as the one on the left) is ideal for working around the yard.

ally occurs when a board isn't set up properly for cutting. As you make the cut, the two parts of the board sag toward each other, pinching the sawblade, which causes the blade to come to a sudden halt and kick back.

To prevent kickback, make sure that the part of the board being cut off is free to fall away. When trimming off a small amount, just let the

end stick out over your sawhorse. When you're cutting through the middle of a board, however, stabilize this setup by placing a weight (such as a concrete block) on the fixed end. As you approach the end of the cut, follow through with a swift, steady push. Otherwise, the weight of the falling piece is liable to split off a part of the remaining board. To guard against surprises, always stand slightly to one side of the cutline. If the saw kicks back, it will go into midair rather than into your groin. Also, be sure that the spring-loaded blade guard is functioning properly.

Using the saw The depth of cut of the saw should be set so that the blade sticks out below the bottom of the board by about the length of one tooth. Putting more blade in the cut just increases friction. Most jobs require an angle adjustment of 90 degrees. Check this occasionally with a square, especially if your butt joints don't seem to be fitting tightly. To cut angles (bevels), tilt the saw's shoe.

Cutting operations can be divided into crosscutting (across the grain), ripping (with the grain), and plywood cutting. To start a freehand cut, align both the sawblade and the guide notch on the saw's shoe with your cutline. (Some saws have two guide notches—one for 90-degree cuts and one for 45-degree bevel cuts.) Back the saw away from the board a little before hitting the trigger. Once you start cutting, it will be hard to watch the blade because so much sawdust will be flying, so steer the saw by the guide notch instead.

You can obtain more accuracy by using cutting guides. For crosscutting, you can hold a Speed Square® against the work to guide the saw. To rip multiple pieces of the same width, use a rip guide. To adjust the rip guide, flip the saw on its back and set the correct distance between the guide's fence and the sawblade. (Make sure the saw is unplugged.)

SUPPORTING STOCK

Cutting between supports is wrong. The board pinches the blade, and kickback can occur.

Free to fall

Trimming an overhanging end is okay.

Cutting through the middle while one half hangs free is okay, but be sure to follow through to avoid splitting.

Counterweight

Circular sawblades come in many patterns, but for landscape carpentry all you really need is a good 24-tooth combination blade. (The word "combination" in this case means that the blade will work equally well for rips, crosscuts, and miters.) Carbide-tipped blades are worth the extra money because of their durability. Special blades for cutting treated wood are available with a nonstick coating, which fights the extra friction caused by wet PT lumber.

As a sawblade becomes dull, it will cut slower, make more noise, and produce a burning smell. Eventually the heat generated by dull teeth will cause the blade to warp, causing even more friction and finally making the blade unusable. Don't let the situation go this far—it increases the risk of kickback and causes premature wear and tear on the tool.

Chopsaws and tablesaws

The chopsaw and tablesaw are two semiportable tools that could come in handy for building some of the projects in this book. For general carpentry work, the chopsaw is especially valuable. In addition to trim, it cuts 2×4s and 2×6s with speed and precision. By turning a board around, you can even cut wider stock. The chopsaw can be mounted on a stand, but for working around the yard it's simpler just to plop it on the ground. To support a long board during a cut, slip a couple of blocks under the end of the board. For safety, don't cut anything less than 6 in. long. If you need a 4-in. piece, for instance, cut it off the end of a longer board.

When shopping for a chopsaw, pay special attention to weight. The lighter the machine, the more useful it will be.

Another semiportable tool that's very handy is the compact tablesaw. Its primary purpose is ripping (cutting with the grain), and it cuts thin strips easily. You can buy a metal stand for the saw,

A motorized chopsaw makes short work of cutting both lumber and trim. Miter cuts, like the one shown here, are as easy as square cuts.

A portable tablesaw is ideal for ripping wide boards into narrow ones. Set the height of the blade so that it protrudes just slightly above the workpiece by about the height of a tooth (the guard has been removed for clarity).

but attaching it to a pair of low sawhorses works just as well.

One of the dangers of using a tablesaw is kickback. This can occur when friction develops between the blade and the workpiece, causing the workpiece to be thrown back toward the operator. Kickback can be caused by accidentally wiggling the workpiece or by a sudden warping of the workpiece as tensions within the board are

WHAT CAN GO WRONG

If the circular saw's spring-loaded blade guard sticks, try spraying it with a penetrating lubricant such as WD-40®. If it still doesn't work right the guard may need a new spring, which can be ordered from a tool repair shop.

released by cutting. To reduce the likelihood of kickback, adjust the blade so that it just clears the work, thereby reducing friction. Never rip boards freehand (without a fence) because even a slight wiggling of the board may cause a kickback.

The worst tablesaw accidents occur when the operator reaches behind the blade to control or retrieve a workpiece. If the workpiece accidentally kicks back at this point, it may drag a hand with it. Just as dangerous is the possibility of a loose sleeve or bracelet catching on the blade. For these reasons, always use a push stick to guide the work past the cut, and have a helper support the work as it exits from the saw so you don't have to reach behind the blade. Whenever you work with a tablesaw, remove any loose jewelry and button your shirt cuffs or roll up your sleeves to the elbow.

As with a chopsaw, weight is the primary consideration when buying a portable tablesaw. Aside from being light, a small tablesaw is easy to stash under a workbench or in a closet. Another important feature of any tablesaw is the rip fence. It should be easy to adjust, and it should stay parallel to the blade without any fussing. A nonparallel rip fence is another potential source of kickback.

Chainsaws

Even small chainsaws are dangerous. Mishandling them can lead to injuries ranging from minor cuts to severe lacerations of the face, shoul-

der, and neck, sometimes causing amputation or death. All tools deserve respect, but when it comes to safety precautions, chainsaws are in a class by themselves.

The good news about chainsaws is that they can quickly cut even large timbers and logs. Gas models are ideal for garden carpentry where electricity isn't available. (Do not use gas models inside, where carbon monoxide exhaust is a hazard.) Another advantage of chainsaws is their versatility. Chainsaws can cut extreme angles beyond the reach of a circular saw, and they can scoop out hollows like a powered carving tool.

When cutting with a chainsaw, keep your thumb curled under the handlebar and your elbows locked.

Avoiding Chainsaw Kickback

LIKE OTHER TYPES OF POWER SAWS, chainsaws are capable of kickback. As the chain races around the bar, it carries terrific momentum with it. If the chain is forced to a sudden stop, a jerk or kick will be the result. This sudden stop can be caused by making accidental contact with another object or the blade being pinched when the workpiece sags in the middle.

Which direction the saw jerks depends on where the chain meets sudden resistance. If resistance occurs on the bottom of the bar, the saw (and the operator) will be tugged toward the workpiece. If resistance occurs on the top of the bar, the saw will be shoved back toward the operator.

Another type of kickback, called rotational kickback, is even more dangerous. It occurs when the chain is suddenly stopped in the upper corner of the bar nose (see the drawing at right). This type of kickback also occurs when the chain is stopped or pinched, but in this case the bar may be thrown up and back toward the operator.

There are a number of ways to guard against kickback. Your first line of defense is to use a low-kickback chain. These safety chains are now standard equipment on homeowner-type saws. Second, don't use the more powerful logging-type chainsaws for carpentry, because the more powerful the saw, the more potent the kickback. Finally, maintain a correct grip and stance, so that the force of a kickback will be automatically resisted by your body. Always keep both hands on the saw. Keep your right hand on the throttle and your left hand on the handlebar, with your left thumb curled underneath the handlebar. Keep your

left arm straight, locked at the elbow, and stand with your legs apart, knees flexed. Above all, stay alert and don't operate a chainsaw when you're tired or upset.

It's advisable to use a bar-nose guard on your chainsaw when doing carpentry work. The guard bolts to the end of the chainsaw bar, virtually eliminating rotational kickback. Bar-nose guards come as original equipment on some saws or can be purchased as an attachment from chainsaw dealers. When starting a chainsaw, keep your right foot inside the handle and your left hand on the handlebar.

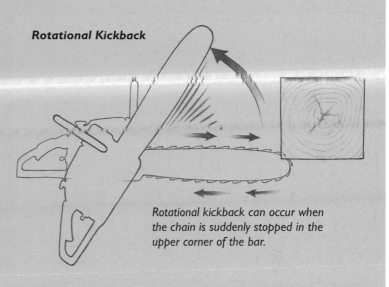

Rotational Kickback

Rotational kickback can occur when the chain is suddenly stopped in the upper corner of the bar.

Wood

Perhaps wood's greatest attraction is its workability. For one thing, wood is relatively light, making it easy to transport and erect. The strength-to-weight ratio of wood is so high that the stuff can be used to build airplanes. As building materials go, wood is also soft. There's a substantial difference between even the hardest of woods and the steel tools and fasteners used to fashion it. This is not the case with other materials. For instance, stone is only slightly softer than hardened tool steel, which makes stonecutting an arduous, drawn-out process. The same is true of metalworking. Having even a little experience with

these stubborn materials will make you appreciate the ease with which a sharp sawblade will slice through a 6×6 timber.

Yet in spite of wood's softness, it is stiff. The strength of wood is most evident in free-spanning members such as floor beams and roof rafters. Metal also has this kind of spanning strength, but it's not as attractive as wood, and masonry has practically no spanning strength. Of course, stone has great compressive strength (the ability to withstand crushing forces), but so does wood. Timber can be stacked into structures such as retaining walls and stairs in much the same

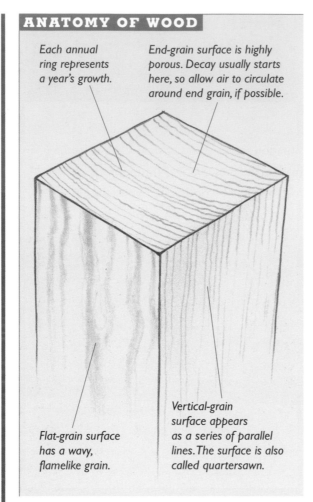

ANATOMY OF WOOD

Each annual ring represents a year's growth.

End-grain surface is highly porous. Decay usually starts here, so allow air to circulate around end grain, if possible.

Flat-grain surface has a wavy, flamelike grain.

Vertical-grain surface appears as a series of parallel lines. The surface is also called quartersawn.

The darker the color of the paint or stain, the more light it will block out, protecting the wood better from decay.

hand, requires meticulous surface preparation and special primers. (Galvanized steel is particularly troublesome to paint.) Plastic won't accept finishes at all, so you're stuck with the original color. The porosity of wood also allows it to be glued effectively, and the new generation of one-part waterproof adhesives makes glue a practical choice for outdoor woodworking.

Problems with using wood outdoors

Wood is a natural material full of idiosyncrasies (see the drawing at left). Those idiosyncrasies are part of wood's great aesthetic appeal, distinguishing it from cold, predictable materials such as metal or plastic. At the same time, wood's "wild side" can create certain headaches for a builder. Wood contains aberrations such as knots and splits that can be thought of as defects or as character, depending on your viewpoint. Wood also has less dimensional stability than other building materials because it expands and contracts, depending on the moisture level of its environment. Finally, wood is prone to decay. Understanding these aspects of wood's personality will help you create structures that look good and perform well over the long haul.

The number-one enemy of wood is moisture. Water, in the presence of oxygen, enables microorganisms to metabolize wood, causing decay. A moist environment is also hospitable to wood-destroying insects such as beetles and carpenter ants. The number-two enemy of wood is sunlight. Sunlight breaks down lignin, the chemical that holds wood cells together.

In the absence of these two enemies, wood can last indefinitely. Wooden objects that are thousands of years old have been found in Egyptian pyramids, preserved by the dark, dry atmosphere of the tombs. Of course, moisture

way that stones or bricks are laid up in masonry, at a fraction of the weight.

Wood also has a trait that is conspicuously absent from metal: visible grain. One piece is never quite identical to another, which allows wood to blend into a living landscape more readily than homogenous materials such as metal or plastic. Wood also weathers in a way that adds to its appearance. The patina of weathered barn boards is easy to warm up to, but rusted iron and cracked plastic are hard to like.

Although the natural look of raw timber is perfect for many garden settings, there may be times when a change of color is desired. In those cases, wood holds paint and stain well by virtue of its porous surface. Metal, on the other

The decay of this column base was helped by its design. The wide horizontal surface caused water to linger, eventually penetrating the end grain of the column and the miter joints of the base. Also, no ventilation was provided to dry up moisture inside the base.

and sunlight are the prime requirements for a healthy garden, so gardeners using wood stand on the front lines of the battle against wood decay.

Decay Wood installed outdoors in a moist climate undergoes a constant cycle of wetting and drying. Not only do rain and snow bombard the wood, but a daily sprinkling of dew also settles on its surface. More water is absorbed into the wood in some places than others, and these points are the first to start decaying. Most susceptible is end grain—the rough surface exposed when a board is cut across the grain. To promote rapid drying, structures should be designed so that as much air as possible circulates around end-grain surfaces.

Horizontal surfaces are also susceptible to wood decay. Although vertical surfaces drain quickly, flat surfaces hold water by a phenomenon known as surface tension. As the water sits, it can soak through paint or water-repellent finishes (see the photo above). To prevent this penetration, horizontal surfaces can be covered with a noncorroding sheet metal, such as copper or aluminum (see the left drawing on p. 16). Another alternative is to design the project without any horizontal surfaces. For instance, deck boards can

be slightly inclined to shed water, whereas surfaces such as handrails and post caps can be beveled (cut on an angle).

Wood that's placed in direct contact with the ground is exposed to moisture constantly. The only effective way to fight decay in that situation is to use wood that contains natural or man-made preservatives throughout.

Unfinished wood that's exposed to intense sunlight will deteriorate into a parched, degraded state known as dry rot (see the photo below). To protect wood from the harsh effects of sunlight, apply a finish. Opaque finishes such as paint or heavy stain offer the best protection.

Insects Wood decay goes hand in hand with wood-destroying insects. As the cellular structure of wood breaks down and decays, various kinds of worms and beetles move in to consume the softened material rapidly. Termites go one step further by eating sound wood as well as rotted wood. Fortunately, the same natural and man-made preservatives that repel decay also repel insects.

Almost all insect attacks start in the ground. For instance, termites tunnel up inside wooden members, leaving an outer shell of wood intact. They must return to the ground periodically,

Exposure to strong sunlight has caused dry rot in these steps.

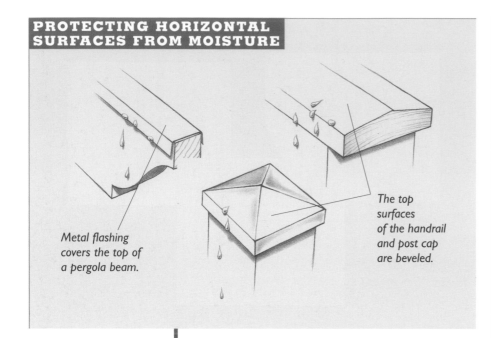

Metal flashing
covers the top of
a pergola beam.

The top
surfaces
of the handrail
and post cap
are beveled.

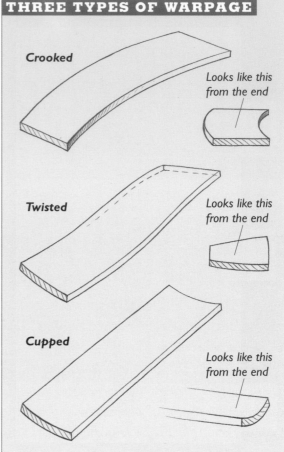

Crooked

Looks like this
from the end

Twisted

Looks like this
from the end

Cupped

Looks like this
from the end

however, to obtain moisture. To create a line of
defense, therefore, all wood that comes in contact
with the ground should have good natural or
man-made decay resistance.

Identifying wood defects

When lumber is sawn out of a log, it is generally
straight. As the lumber dries out, it shrinks. This
can cause various kinds of warping (as shown in
the right drawings above). There are also natural
defects in the wood to consider, such as knots,
pith, and wane.

Crook and twist A board that bends along its
length while remaining flat is said to be crooked,
whereas a board that warps in three dimensions
simultaneously is called twisted. Both types
should be avoided. To detect these deformities in
a board, pick up one end and sight down along
its edge (see the right drawings above).

Crook and twist occur when natural tensions
that develop in a growing tree are released by
cutting and drying. More of these tensions exist
in young, rapidly growing trees than in mature,
slow-growing trees. Knowing this can help you

avoid boards that are apt to warp as they dry.
When you pick out lumber, look at the ends of
the boards (see the photo on the facing page).
When growth rings are tightly spaced, it means
the tree grew slowly in a dark forest. These
boards tend to remain stable. If the rings are far
apart, the tree grew rapidly in a free-for-all with
other young trees groping for light. These boards
are weak and unstable.

Cupping When a board is curved in on one
face and curved out on the opposite face, it is
cupped. Cupping occurs when a board shrinks
more on one side than on the other. To detect
cupping, sight across the end of a board or lay
a straightedge across the board's face.

Splitting and checking When shrinkage
occurs too rapidly, boards tend to split (see the

drawing at right). The worst splitting occurs on the ends of boards, which dry out quickly as the water that's there is wicked away by evaporation. Although the last few inches of the board shrink radically, the wood farther from the end remains swollen. Finally, as tension increases, the end of the board is torn apart.

Rapid drying can also cause splitting on the face of a board, usually to a lesser extent than on the ends. These defects, called face checks, often don't weaken the board structurally, but they can be unsightly. Checks provide a point of entry for moisture, which sometimes leads to decay, especially on horizontal surfaces.

Knots, pith, and wane Knots are cylinders of hardened tissue formed in the trunk of a tree where branches are located. The way in which a board is sliced from a log dictates how a given knot will appear on the board's surface (see the drawing on p. 18). If the face of a board is oriented perpendicular to the axis of a knot, the knot will show up as a round knot. If the face of a board cuts parallel to the knot, it will appear long and slender—a spike knot.

When selecting knotty boards, pay special attention to large, round knots. When dried rapidly, these knots may become loose. If a continuous crack has developed around a knot, it is liable to fall out over time. Knots also contain resins that invariably bleed through paint and stain,

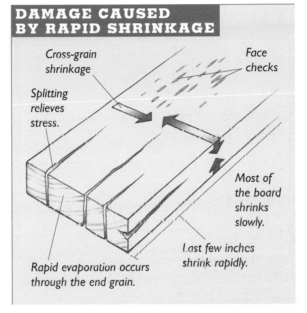

DAMAGE CAUSED BY RAPID SHRINKAGE

Cross-grain shrinkage

Face checks

Splitting relieves stress.

Most of the board shrinks slowly.

Last few inches shrink rapidly.

Rapid evaporation occurs through the end grain.

appearing as dark shadows on the surface. The problem is especially noticeable with a light-colored finish.

Pith is the weak tissue formed in a young sapling's first few years of growth. It is found in boards cut from the very center of a log. Pith is apt to split and peel when exposed to the weather.

Wane is an irregular absence of wood along a board's edge. It occurs when the natural outside of a log falls within the trimmed width of the board.

Whether you avoid these defects depends on your design intentions. If a smooth, painted surface is your goal, you should invest in clear

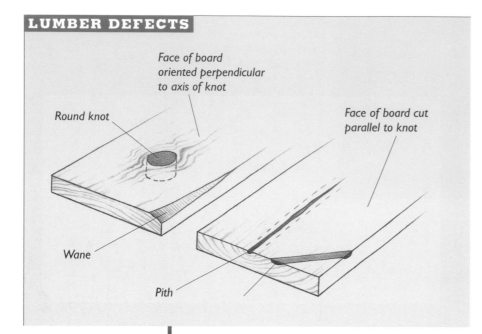

Round knot

Face of board oriented perpendicular to axis of knot

Face of board cut parallel to knot

Wane

Pith

(defect-free) boards. For rustic projects, you can save money by buying lower-grade lumber, appreciating its irregularity as a token of its natural origins.

Seasoning wood

To reduce splitting and warping, softwoods should be seasoned: gradually dried until their moisture content is in equilibrium with the environment in which the wood will be used. Unseasoned lumber is said to be "green," a term referring not to the actual color of the wood but to the greenness of the tree from which it was recently cut. Pressure-treated lumber, which is also sometimes referred to as "green" because of its characteristic color, may be seasoned or unseasoned. Yet a third type of "green" wood is that which has been harvested in an ecologically responsible way.

To season the wood, stack the boards in a shady place with 1-in.-thick sticks between each layer of boards (see the photo on the facing page). Cover the stack with plywood or sheet metal, leaving the sides of the pile exposed. The covering will keep out rain and sun. In dry summer weather, seasoning of green softwood lumber takes as little as two weeks, but in winter it may take several months to reach moisture equilibrium.

Although fresh-cut softwoods should always be seasoned, hardwoods such as oak are another story. Hardwoods tend to experience a very high degree of warping and splitting as they dry, even under ideal conditions. Once they are dry, they become so hard that they are difficult to work with. For outdoor work, it's better to use hardwoods in the green state and let them dry in place. A lot of shrinkage and a certain degree of checking will occur, but that's better than trying to work with lumber that is cupped, twisted, and hard as nails.

Some construction lumber is dried in a kiln before it is sold, and it can be used outdoors immediately. It will be marked "KD" (for kiln-dried). PT lumber is dried initially, but it is then pumped full of water to convey chemical preservatives into the wood. Some PT lumber is redried after it's treated, but most of it is sold wet (which is why it's so heavy). Seasoning this saturated lumber before use greatly improves the quality of your finished product.

Choosing wood

Choosing the right type of wood for your outdoor project can be confusing. There are, after all, literally thousands of wood products available for landscape carpentry (characteristics of a few types of wood are listed in the chart on p. 177). One of your first considerations should be workability, which depends mostly on the wood's hardness. Hardwoods are more difficult to work with than softwoods, especially if you're limited to the use of hand tools. Another prime consideration is decay resistance. There are two broad

categories of decay-resistant lumber: those that grow naturally and those that are impregnated with preservative chemicals.

The size and shape of the material you need may restrict your choice of wood species because different trees grow in different sizes. Also, your geographical location may determine what's available locally. In some cases, technology has circumvented these restrictions by synthesizing larger and/or more durable wood products from small, nondurable trees.

Lumber can be milled in different ways. Because landscape carpentry is often massive and rustic in nature, it lends itself to the use of large beams and poles. These range from smooth-planed timbers to coarse, round logs, with many variations in between. You'll have to make a lot of decisions about what wood is best for your project. For more on choosing wood, see Appendix 2 on p. 176.

Outdoor Fasteners

One of the most important decisions you'll have to make about your project is what fasteners to use. You'll have to balance the need for strength against aesthetic concerns. For instance, a large bolt that might look right at home on a heavy timber project would spoil the looks of a lacy trellis—and be unnecessary to boot. Conversely, you wouldn't use light finish nails to join 4×4s together—they simply wouldn't hold. As you gain experience with different fasteners, you will develop an intuitive sense of what works and what doesn't.

Nails

Nails come in a bewildering array of sizes, finishes, and types. The size of nails is generally measured by the penny, an arcane unit of weight. To complicate matters further, penny is abbreviated as "d" after a Roman coin called a denarius. Most lumberyards have a chart on the wall to help you translate the length of a nail into pennyweight (see the drawing on p. 20). The length of a nail should be at least twice the thickness of the piece being fastened, although three times the thickness is ideal.

Most nails are made of mild steel. For outdoor work, steel nails are galvanized, meaning that they are coated with a layer of noncorroding zinc. Steel nails that have not been galvanized

Lumber is seasoned by removing excess moisture. To promote air circulation and drying, place sticks between the boards. Cover the stack with sheets of plywood.

TRADE SECRET

To ensure quality, look for the label of a reputable preservative manufacturer when you buy pressure-treated lumber. Some companies, such as Osmose, have a national reputation that you can depend on. Other products are best known by a popular brand name, such as Wolmanized.

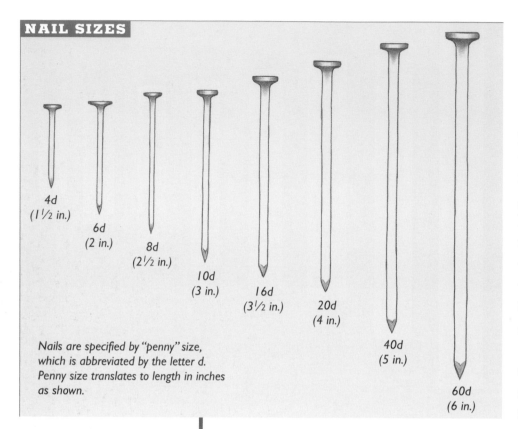

4d
(1½ in.)

6d
(2 in.)

8d
(2½ in.)

10d
(3 in.)

16d
(3½ in.)

20d
(4 in.)

40d
(5 in.)

60d
(6 in.)

Nails are specified by "penny" size, which is abbreviated by the letter d. Penny size translates to length in inches as shown.

PROTIP

As a substitute for spikes, you can use lengths of concrete reinforcing bar (called rebar) to fasten timbers together. Preferably the rebar should be heavily galvanized to resist corrosion, especially for use with PT timbers.

Finish nails have very small heads, which makes for a neat appearance. Galvanized finish nails can be driven flush with the surface, or they can be punched below the surface. The hole can then be filled with caulk or glazing compound prior to painting. Finish nails bend more easily than common nails because they are skinnier. Bending doesn't occur much in soft, even-grained woods such as cedar or redwood, but in a hard, stringy wood such as PT yellow pine, finish nails are difficult to drive. Another problem is that the small head of a finish nail cannot restrain unstable types of wood from warping. As the board warps, it simply slips past the finish nail's tiny head.

Special-purpose nails are available for particular applications. One type, called a deck nail, is designed specifically for installing PT decking. It's heavier than a finish nail, with a larger head, but not as beefy as a common nail. This combination makes it easy to drive yet discreet in appearance. Deck nails also have a spiral twist, which provides greater holding power. Siding nails are similar to deck nails but slightly skinnier.

Screws

The development of powerful cordless drills in recent years has made the use of screws more and more popular. Screws have two main advantages over nails: First, they have much greater holding power than nails. Second, screws can be removed easily, which makes fixing mistakes a lot easier.

Along with better screw-driving tools have come improvements in screws themselves. Old-fashioned wood screws have a thick, tapering shank. These screws work fine, but they require that two different sizes of pilot holes be drilled to avoid splitting the wood. Although old-fashioned tapered screws are available in plated steel, brass, or stainless steel, only stainless-steel screws offer

are referred to as "bright." They should not be used outdoors. As a substitute for galvanized nails, stainless-steel nails are available in many shapes and sizes. Because they are noncorroding through and through, these nails are ideal for outdoor use, and they won't stain, as galvanized nails sometimes do. The only drawback of stainless-steel nails is their high cost.

Nails can be divided into four broad categories: spikes, common nails, finish nails, and special-purpose nails (see the top drawing on the facing page). Spikes range from 6 in. to 12 in. in length. They're used to fasten heavy timbers together.

Common nails run from 1½ in. to 6 in. long (4d to 60d). They are fairly stout in relation to their length, making them easy to drive. Galvanized common nails are good all-purpose fasteners for outdoor carpentry.

maximum corrosion resistance and longevity. For high-end projects, stainless-steel screws are worth the extra cost.

In recent years, the tapered screw has given way to a newer style generically referred to as outdoor screws, or deck screws. Outdoor screws are patterned after their indoor cousin, the black "drywall screw." Like drywall screws, outdoor screws have a straight, slender shank that can penetrate most substrates without a pilot hole. A clearance hole in the part being fastened is all that's necessary. In very soft wood, it's even possible to drive these screws through both pieces without predrilling any hole whatsoever. One style of outdoor screw has a chisel point that drills its own hole as the screw is driven. These "self-drilling" screws are somewhat more expensive than regular pointed screws, but they save time.

Outdoor screws have one drawback when compared to old-fashioned tapered screws. Because outdoor screws are skinnier, they have less shear strength (the ability to withstand forces that are applied sideways to the screw's axis). In cases where heavy shear loads are to be applied, tapered screws may be preferable to the skinnier outdoor screws. For most garden projects, however, outdoor screws will work fine.

Lag bolts

Lag bolts are really overgrown screws (see the left drawing on p. 22). They have a hex head that is driven by a wrench instead of a screwdriver for greater leverage. Lag bolts are available from ¼ in. to ¾ in. in diameter and up to 12 in. long. They do the same work as spikes, but they have much greater holding power.

Washers are used under a lag bolt's head to keep it from digging in during tightening. Washers also spread the pressure of the bolt head

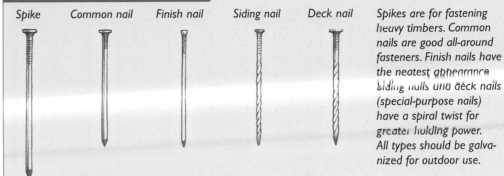

NAILS FOR OUTDOORS

Spike · Common nail · Finish nail · Siding nail · Deck nail

Spikes are for fastening heavy timbers. Common nails are good all-around fasteners. Finish nails have the neatest appearance. Siding nails and deck nails (special-purpose nails) have a spiral twist for greater holding power. All types should be galvanized for outdoor use.

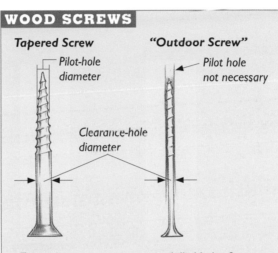

WOOD SCREWS

Tapered Screw · "Outdoor Screw"

Pilot-hole diameter · Pilot hole not necessary

Clearance-hole diameter

Tapered screws require two predrilled holes for proper installation, but outdoor screws require only one.

Phillips · Slotted · Square

Phillips-head screws are easier to drive than slotted screws. Square-drive screws are even easier.

PRO TIP

Wood-polymer decking has a tendency to "mushroom" around the head of a screw that's driven into it. A special type of deck screw with an irregular thread can overcome this problem.

PRO TIP

Before buying screws, inspect the drive recesses in their heads. In poorly galvanized screws, the drive recesses fill up with zinc, making the screws difficult to drive. To avoid this problem altogether, buy stainless-steel screws.

over a wider area. Otherwise, the wood under the head of the bolt will gradually be crushed, causing the joint to loosen over time.

Through-bolts

Through-bolts (see the right drawing on p. 22) pass completely through both pieces being fastened and are tightened with a nut and washer (unlike lag bolts, which pass completely through one piece but only partway into the other). One

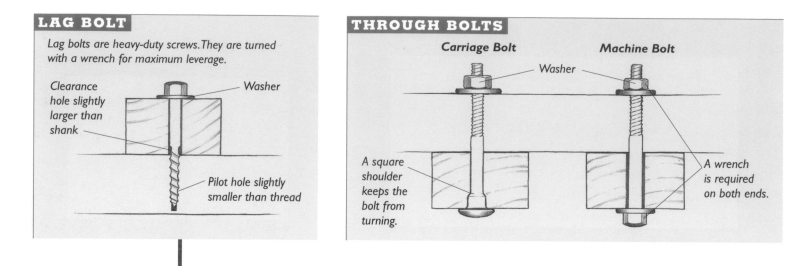

Lag bolts are heavy-duty screws. They are turned with a wrench for maximum leverage.

Clearance hole slightly larger than shank

Washer

Pilot hole slightly smaller than thread

Carriage Bolt

Machine Bolt

Washer

A square shoulder keeps the bolt from turning.

A wrench is required on both ends.

WHAT CAN GO WRONG

When CCA-treated lumber was replaced by the new compounds ACQ and CA, it was soon discovered that the new chemicals were more corrosive to metal fasteners than CCA. When you buy galvanized fasteners or framing hardware for use with PT lumber, make sure they are heavily galvanized, indicated by a rating of G-185. An even better but more expensive alternative is stainless-steel fasteners.

type of through-bolt, called a carriage bolt, has a round head with a square shoulder just below it. The corners of the shoulder bite into the surrounding wood to keep the bolt from turning while its nut is being tightened. Another type of bolt, called a machine bolt, has a hex head that is gripped with a second wrench while the nut is being tightened.

Carriage bolts work well in seasoned wood because the wood is hard enough to resist the turning action of the bolt's shoulder. The nut should be tightened until the washer under the nut just starts to crush into the wood surface. In soft, moist wood, the shoulder of a carriage bolt is apt to slip during tightening. In those cases it's better to use a machine bolt.

Framing connectors

Special-purpose framing connectors produce joints of great tenacity by applying the tremendous tensile strength of steel over a broad area around the joint (see the drawings on the facing page). In contrast, nails and screws "capture" only small amounts of wood under their heads. When a nail or screwed joint fails, it is often these small captured areas close to the end of a board that give way, not the fasteners themselves.

Unfortunately, most framing hardware has an industrial appearance that is ill-suited to garden architecture. One way to amend this is to paint your framing connectors a dark color. Wait a year or so after installing them on your project before painting to allow the galvanized surface of the connectors to weather, as new galvanized steel does not hold paint.

Adhesives

Outdoor adhesives come in the form of liquid glues or caulk-type construction adhesives. Construction adhesives are easy to apply and some are formulated to bond under less-than-ideal conditions, including wet or frozen wood. However, they aren't as strong as some of the liquid glues.

The best all-around outdoor glue is liquid glue formulated for exterior use that requires no mixing (the leading brand is Titebond III). This type of glue can stand up to rain, sleet, and snow, and can even withstand some immersion.

Two-part glues that require mixing are also used outdoors. Epoxies are often sold in syringes that automatically dispense the correct amounts of each part. They set up very quickly, as fast as five minutes, and don't require much clamping pressure. Another two-part glue, resorcinol, offers the highest water resistance of all. It can be submerged underwater indefinitely without losing its grip. Resorcinol comes as a liquid, with a powdered catalyst that acts as a hardener. Polyurethane glues are a recent development. They are strong and waterproof but are rather expensive. Polyurethane glues work especially well with wet, unseasoned wood because the glue is actually activated by water. Other types of glue become diluted on wet wood, reducing their holding power.

Outdoor Finishes

Finishes can change the appearance of your project. They can also inhibit deterioration by keeping out water and ultraviolet (UV) light. When choosing a finish, you must weigh these potential benefits against the long-term costs of maintaining a finish in good condition.

Water repellents and preservatives

Water repellents are clear finishes that reduce some of the more drastic effects of weathering, such as warping and splitting, yet still allow wood to turn to its natural gray color. The principal ingredient in water repellents is wax, which is dissolved in an oil/solvent mixture that conveys the wax onto the wood surface. After water repellent has been applied, water will bead up on a wood surface as it does on a freshly waxed automobile (see the photo on p. 24). After a few months, the beading action dissipates, but the wood continues to absorb less water than it would without treatment. However, water-repellent finishes are short-lived in comparison to other finishes. Depending on the degree of exposure, they must be renewed every one to three years to remain effective.

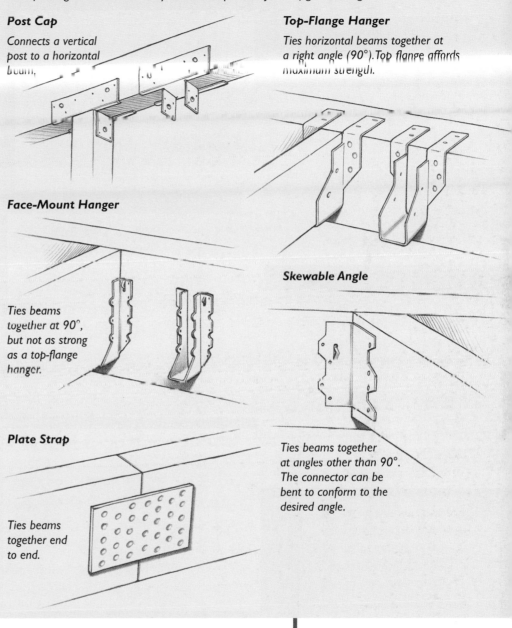

FRAMING CONNECTORS

Steel framing connectors are easy to use and produce joints of great strength.

Post Cap
Connects a vertical post to a horizontal beam.

Top-Flange Hanger
Ties horizontal beams together at a right angle (90°). Top flange affords maximum strength.

Face-Mount Hanger
Ties beams together at 90°, but not as strong as a top-flange hanger.

Skewable Angle
Ties beams together at angles other than 90°. The connector can be bent to conform to the desired angle.

Plate Strap
Ties beams together end to end.

In addition to wax, most water repellents contain a fungicide, which boosts decay resistance and controls mildew. This type of finish is known as a water-repellent preservative. Although it can prolong the life of above-ground wood if maintained regularly, it offers nowhere near the effectiveness of pressure treatment. Applying

TRADE SECRET

Before rushing at your project with a paint-brush, consider leaving it alone. Wood that has natural or man-made decay resistance can be left without a finish for a rustic, weathered appearance. Even not-so-decay-resistant species will last a long time without a finish, provided there is plenty of air circulation around them to keep moisture below the decay threshold. This option may be especially appealing if you are growing edibles on the structure and you would prefer not to grow your food near any chemically treated wood.

A wax-based water repellent causes water to bead on this freshly coated surface.

water-repellent preservatives to below-grade wood, such as fence posts, is a waste of time.

Most water repellents can be painted over. The water repellent acts as a primer, reducing the amount of paint that is initially absorbed into the wood. Because water repellents are easy to apply, they are often used as a temporary finish to protect new work from the immediate harsh effects of rain and sun. The water repellent gives interim protection until paint can be applied.

Varnishes

Varnishes are clear finishes that form a surface film rather than penetrating into the wood like water repellent. Varnishes are mainly used on smooth wood to accentuate color and grain.

The best varnish for exterior use is marine spar varnish, which is formulated to have a high degree of elasticity to help it withstand extremes of temperature and moisture. Unfortunately, even marine spar varnish offers only short-lived protection. Varnishes exposed to sunlight usually crack and start peeling within two years, and the old varnish must be completely sanded off before refinishing. Varnishes also offer little protection against UV degradation because they contain no pigments. The only exterior projects that are suitable for a varnish are those that are at least partially shaded by some sort of overhang.

Semitransparent penetrating stains

Penetrating stains are similar to water repellents, except that they contain pigments. Pigments reduce the penetration of UV light, thereby protecting the wood as well as prolonging the life of the finish itself. Penetrating stains should only be applied over new wood or previous coats of water-repellent or penetrating stain. Previous coats of paint or heavy-bodied stain will block the absorption of penetrating stain into the surface.

Penetrating stains are effective for a natural look. Pigment helps to obscure more prominent defects, such as knots and checks, but lets some of the wood grain show through. Penetrating stains do a particularly good job of hiding defects on roughsawn surfaces, because a coarse-textured surface drinks up more finish than a smooth-planed surface does. Increased absorption also makes the finish last longer. Penetrating stains can last as long as eight years on roughsawn surfaces, whereas four years is about the limit on smooth-planed work.

One of the biggest advantages of penetrating stains is that they do not crack or peel like film-forming finishes (such as varnishes) do. That means no more scraping in preparation for recoating. To prepare for restaining, the wood needs to be brushed clean with a wire brush, then hosed off.

Solid-color stains

Although called stain, this product is essentially a thin, flat paint. Most of these stains are latex or acrylic based and are formulated somewhat thinner than regular paints so that more surface texture will show through the finish. Like paint, solid-color stains (also called opaque stains) form a surface film that will eventually peel. Because solid-color stains contain less pigment than paint, their life is proportionally reduced. Although paint systems are expected to last 7 to 10 years, solid-color stains last only 3 to 7 years. One advantage of solid-color stains is that they can be applied over previous film-forming finishes. They can also be applied over old penetrating finishes, as long as the surface is sanded first to remove surface oils.

Paints

No surface treatment can alter a project as dramatically as a coat of paint. White paint is the tried-and-true favorite for setting off an arbor or fence against a landscape. Colors are also effective at relating structures to nearby architecture.

Practically speaking, paint finishes provide the best protection against UV light because of their high concentration of pigments. (Dark colors offer more protection than lighter colors.) Paints also block the absorption of water better than other finishes, but this is a two-edged sword. Once moisture does penetrate a painted surface, the paint tends to hold that moisture inside, which can cause premature decay, especially of end grain. For that reason, surfaces that are exposed to standing water for long periods of time, such as decks, are better treated with a "breathable" finish such as a water-repellent or penetrating stain.

As a wood surface dries and swells, or heats up and cools down, the paint film is subjected to a great deal of stress, so paint with good elasticity works the best. Although oil-based paints are prized for their sealing ability, they are not as elastic as latex paints. Latex paints stretch well and even have the ability to span over minor cracks in the wood surface or in the primer coat. Based on these pros and cons, a good plan for

This gate is visually tied to the house behind it by the color of its paint.

exterior paint is one coat of oil-based primer followed by two latex-based top coats. As technology improves, oil-based paints will probably fade from the scene altogether.

When shopping for paint, look at the solids content listed on the label. Solids are the only part of the paint that remains on the surface permanently; the solvents used to deliver the solids will evaporate. A 50-percent solids paint that costs only 5 percent more than a 40-percent solids paint is a better buy. When comparing latex paints, look for an all-acrylic binder, which is superior to a vinyl binder.

BUILDING
OUTDOORS

So you've got your working drawings and your building permit, and the lumber was dumped off in your driveway yesterday. You're ready to start building. But before the sawdust starts flying, it pays to study a few how-to basics that are common to many kinds of garden structures.

Different structures require different types of construction. Frame construction is a way of joining individual parts into a frame or skeleton. Frame construction stands apart from "log-cabin" building techniques, which simply stack horizontal timbers in a way that's similar to masonry. For garden projects, you'll commonly use one of two types of frame construction: pole construction or timber-frame construction.

Beyond the type of construction, you'll need to determine your structure's finish. A finish can protect the project from weather and contribute to its look. ▶ ▶ ▶

1 Frame Construction
p. 28

2 Pole Construction
p. 32

3 Timber Framing
p. 40

4 Finishing Techniques
p. 42

Frame Construction

For thousands of years, woodworkers relied on nothing more than carefully wrought joints to hold buildings and furniture together. Today, nails and screws make it possible to join wooden members together with much less trouble. Metal framing connectors produce joints that are as strong as the most sophisticated mortise-and-tenon joint. In some cases, metal fasteners can also add an interesting accent, such as iron bolts used in heavy timber construction.

However, despite the benefits of fasteners, joinery gives a more integrated look than metal fasteners alone (see the left drawing below). A half-lap joint, for instance, will keep the faces of two adjoining members flush (in the same plane). If the members were overlapped and bolted, there would be a visual disruption at the joint, which might not look as nice. If the members were simply butted and nailed, the joint would be flush but not very strong.

To create the best frame construction, fasteners and joinery should be used together (see the right drawing below). For instance, a cross member that was simply nailed to a post would fail as soon as the nails started to pull loose, whereas a cross member that was fastened with a joint as well as nails would have direct wood-to-wood support. In that case, the nails don't carry weight—they merely hold the cross member in place.

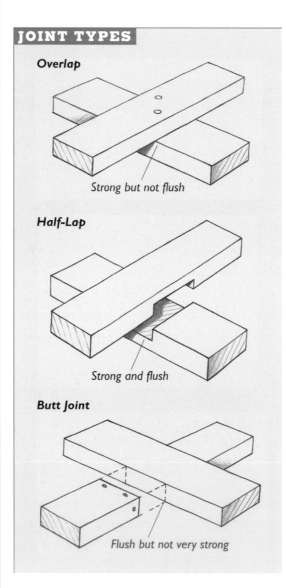

JOINT TYPES

Overlap

Strong but not flush

Half-Lap

Strong and flush

Butt Joint

Flush but not very strong

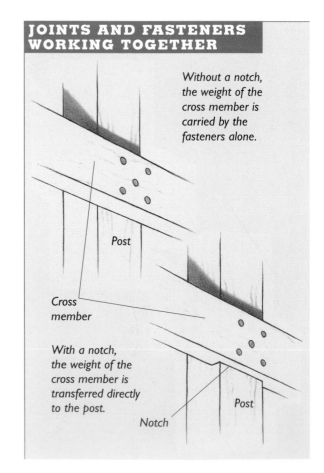

JOINTS AND FASTENERS WORKING TOGETHER

Without a notch, the weight of the cross member is carried by the fasteners alone.

Post

Cross member

With a notch, the weight of the cross member is transferred directly to the post.

Notch

Post

Butt joints

A butt joint is really not a joint at all. One piece of wood simply butts into another. The strength of a butt joint depends entirely on the fasteners used. The joint is usually reinforced with nails driven at an angle—a process called toenailing (see the drawing below). The nails should penetrate at roughly a 45-degree angle, with half the length of the nail ending up in each member.

To create a stronger butt joint, you can substitute screws for nails. A screw will go in better if the starting hole in the piece being attached is slightly bigger than the screw. You don't need friction between a screw and its clearance hole because the clamping action of the screw's head does all the work.

Glue is ineffective for reinforcing butt joints because one of the mating surfaces will be an end-grain surface. End grain is so porous that it will immediately soak up any glue that's applied to it. The joint will therefore be starved for glue, making it weak.

Notches in this post help support the adjoining corner braces, taking most of the strain off the lag bolts used to secure the joints.

Notching

Notching allows one piece to be partially "let in" to another (see the photo above). It is especially effective for joining horizontal cross members, such as fence rails, to vertical posts (see the right drawing on the facing page). By notching the post, a shoulder is created for the rail to sit on.

Notches in main structural members shouldn't be deeper than necessary or they will weaken the post. In the case of fence rails, a notch only ½ in. deep in a 4×4 post will provide plenty of bearing for the rail without greatly weakening the post.

1. To cut a notch, begin by marking it on the piece using a pencil and a combination square, as shown in **A** on p. 30. If similar notches are to be cut in other pieces, such as a set of four corner posts, you can line up all the pieces side by side and mark all the notches at once.

2. After marking the faces of the notches on all four pieces, square down (draw perpendicular lines) on the sides of each piece to mark the

PRO**TIP**

To make toenailing easier and to prevent splitting, you can drill pilot holes in the piece being attached. The diameter of the holes should be slightly smaller than the diameter of the nail for a snug fit.

FASTENING BUTT JOINTS

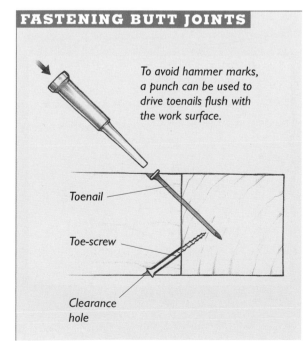

To avoid hammer marks, a punch can be used to drive toenails flush with the work surface.

Toenail

Toe-screw

Clearance hole

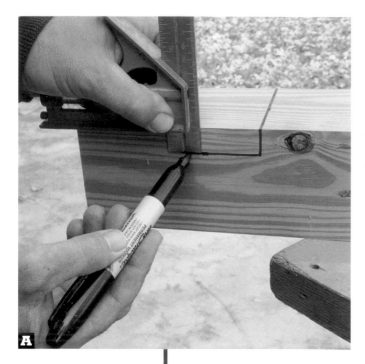

shoulders. To mark the bottom of the notch, set your combination square to the depth of the notch and slide it along from one shoulder to the other, holding a pencil or a marker against the end of the square's blade.

3. Now make sawcuts at each shoulder down to the bottom of the notch. You can use a circular saw or a handsaw for this. If you're using a circular saw, you'll need to adjust the depth of cut. Make a few trial cuts in a test piece to make sure you have it right.

4. After cutting the shoulders of the notch, you'll need to remove the wood between the shoulders. Start with a series of crosscuts almost as deep as the shoulder cuts. Take a chisel and split out most of the waste material as shown in **B**. The crosscuts allow most of the waste to come out easily in little pieces.

5. With the bulk of the material removed, pare the remaining wood down to the line with

a chisel. Keep the flat side of the chisel down and work toward the center from the outside. Work at about a 45-degree angle to the direction of the grain, slicing off thin wafers of wood until you reach the bottom of the notch.

Lap joints

Lap joints are good, simple joints for garden carpentry (see the drawings on the facing page). Once you have mastered notches, lap joints will be almost as easy. A lap joint is similar to a notched joint, except that both pieces are notched instead of one. When they overlap, the two pieces are flush.

To make a lap joint, notch one piece to a depth of half its thickness. Then lay it on top of the other piece and use the notched piece as a template to mark the shoulders of the notch on the second piece. Nails, screws, or bolts can be used to hold the pieces together; glue also greatly increases the strength of the joint.

Notching an End

WHEN MAKING A NOTCH on the end of a piece, such as for a T half-lap joint, you can saw the waste material off in one piece rather than chiseling out the waste. To do this, saw the shoulder cut, then turn the piece on edge and start the lengthwise cut. Hold the saw at a 45-degree angle so you can eyeball the cutline on the end of the stock as well as on the edge. If you have a vise at your disposal, clamp the workpiece at an angle to gain a more comfortable stance (see the photo at right). After you have sawn the lengthwise cut about halfway through, flip the piece around and saw in from the opposite edge as well. Keep cutting down until you reach the shoulder cut and the waste drops off.

LAP JOINTS

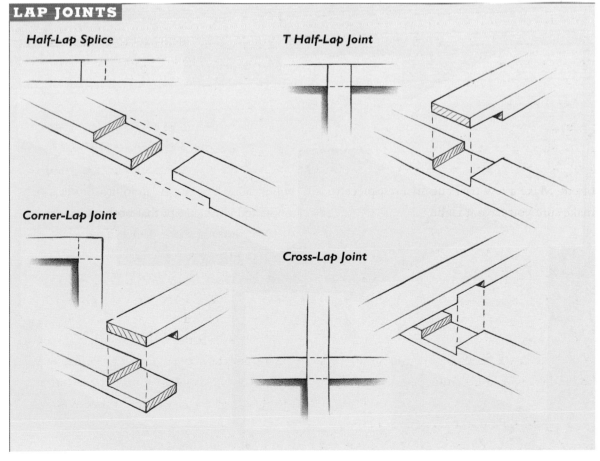

Half-Lap Splice

T Half-Lap Joint

Corner-Lap Joint

Cross-Lap Joint

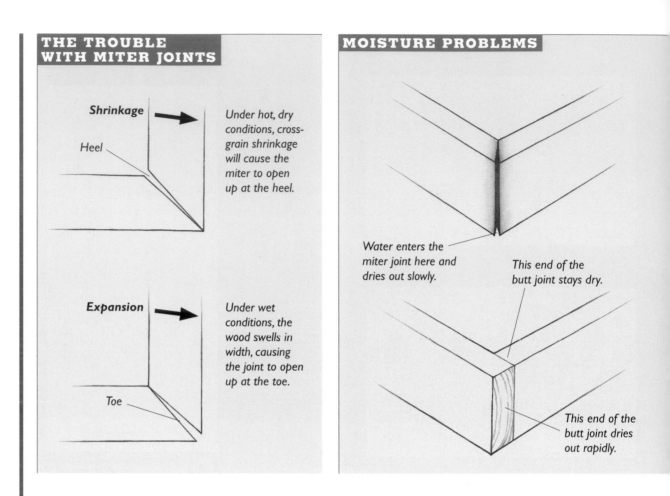

Shrinkage

Heel

Under hot, dry conditions, cross-grain shrinkage will cause the miter to open up at the heel.

Expansion

Toe

Under wet conditions, the wood swells in width, causing the joint to open up at the toe.

Water enters the miter joint here and dries out slowly.

This end of the butt joint stays dry.

This end of the butt joint dries out rapidly.

Miter joints

Two tapering ends joined together create a miter joint. Most miter joints are cut at a 45-degree angle to produce a square corner. They are used a lot indoors for appearance's sake because they hide the rough end-grain surface of a board. Unfortunately, miter joints don't work very well in outdoor carpentry for two reasons (see the left drawings above).

First, outdoor miter joints invariably open up due to wide fluctuations in dampness. The wider the boards, the more pronounced these gaps will be.

The second problem with miter joints is that, because of seasonal fluctuations, water invariably enters the joint, where it's absorbed by the end grain. The end grain is mostly concealed and less air circulation reaches it, so the wood dries out

slowly, leading to decay (see the right drawings above).

If a miter joint must be used, pin it together with nails or screws. This won't stop the shrinking and swelling, but it will at least hold the two pieces in alignment. Be sure to drill pilot holes. Not only will the holes prevent splitting, but they will also reduce the tendency of mitered pieces to slide against each other as they are fastened.

Pole Construction

Lightweight standing structures such as arbors, pergolas, and fences are typically built with pole construction. In pole construction, the primary vertical members (square posts or round poles) bear directly on soil, without the benefit of a masonry foundation (see the drawings below). That means a pole-type structure requires much less digging than a conventionally built structure such as a house. In addition, the cost of a masonry foundation is saved. Pole structures are limited in weight, however, because their mass is concentrated on a relatively small area of ground. Too much weight can cause a pole structure to settle, especially when built on soft, compressible soil. Pole construction is more than adequate for most garden structures, but if you have something monumental in mind, you should consult an architect or a structural engineer to see if a masonry foundation is needed.

Laying out a pole structure

A pole structure begins as a series of holes in the ground. Locating these holes is a two-step process. The first step is to establish the structure's essential building lines. The second step is to locate individual posts in relation to these lines.

For a straight fence, there is only one building line to worry about: a straight line drawn between two stakes. If the fence changes direction, stakes will be needed at each turning point. But for a three-dimensional structure, such as a pergola, the structure's footprint needs to be staked out. In most cases, the footprint will consist of a rectangle or a series of connected rectangles.

POLE CONSTRUCTION VERSUS MASONRY FOUNDATION CONSTRUCTION

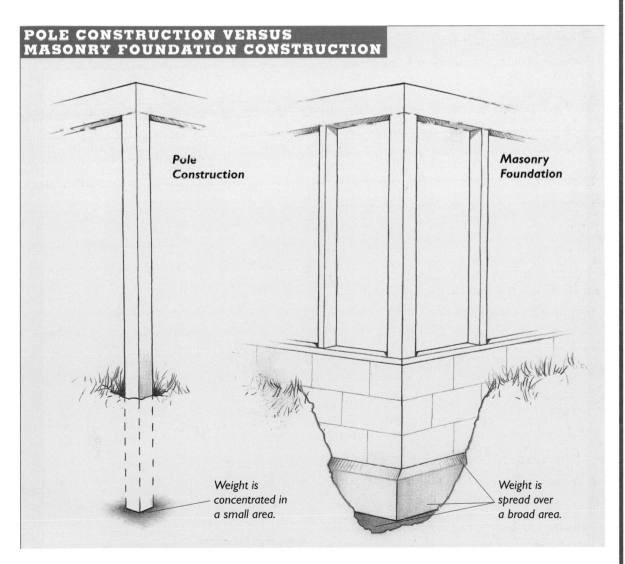

Pole Construction

Masonry Foundation

Weight is concentrated in a small area.

Weight is spread over a broad area.

Of course other, more ambitious shapes are also possible, including triangles, circles, and octagons (see p. 155).

Rectangular footprints need to be truly square, meaning all corners must be 90 degrees. Taking pains to make things perfect at this early stage will pay dividends throughout the rest of the building process. When a structure is out of square, measurements become confusing, cuts don't line up right, and everything becomes more difficult.

If you have a sheet of plywood on hand, the easiest way to lay out a square footprint for a structure that measures 4 ft. by 8 ft. or less is to make a template for the entire structure. As long as you make your template square, your layout will be square as well. To make things simple, you can use plywood, hardboard (such as Masonite), or even gypsum board. These products are manufactured square in the first place, which will give you a head start. Lay the template on the ground and spray-paint around its edges. When you remove the sheet, a "shadow" will indicate the building lines.

To lay out footprints that are larger than 4 ft. by 8 ft., you can use string. In the case of a rectangle, begin by driving four corner pins or wooden stakes. The distance between the pins or stakes must be equal on opposing sides of the rectangle, but a rectangle's diagonal measurements must also be equal for the rectangle to be square. If one diagonal is longer than the other, the layout must be shifted so that the long diagonal shrinks and the short diagonal stretches (see the drawings below). When the diagonals agree, your layout is correct.

Once the structure's footprint has been established, locate the actual post holes. First, make a cardboard template according to the post's dimensions (for instance, 3½ in. by 3½ in. for a 4×4 post). A scrap block of the same size lumber used for the post can be used instead of a template. Set the template or block in position, with its outside edges on the building line, then paint a circle around the template to indicate the hole itself (see the left photo on the facing page). The diameter of the hole should be two to three times the width of the post (i.e., 8 in. to 12 in. for a 4×4). The same process must be repeated to locate posts between corners or when the footprint consists of multiple rectangles.

CHECKING A FOOTPRINT FOR SQUARE

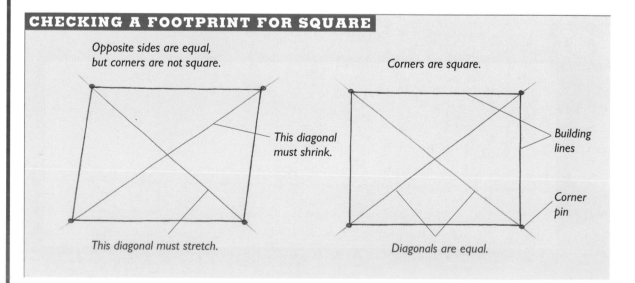

Opposite sides are equal, but corners are not square.

This diagonal must shrink.

This diagonal must stretch.

Corners are square.

Building lines

Corner pin

Diagonals are equal.

To simulate the position of a post, set a block with one corner touching a layout pin where the building lines intersect. Draw a circle around the block to indicate the location of the post hole.

Digging post holes

Post holes can be dug mechanically or by hand, and their depth depends on a few variables (see the sidebar at right).

Augers The easiest way is with a mechanical auger mounted on the back of a tractor (see the photo at right). The auger is raised and lowered hydraulically by a hitch on the back of the tractor, and the rotation of the auger is driven by the tractor's PTO (power takeoff). Two operators are required—one to work the tractor and another to position the auger. With such power and stability, large-diameter holes can be dug quickly, even in rocky soils. If you're contemplating a large project, ask around about tractors. Farmers,

Depth of Post Holes

IT'S DIFFICULT TO MAKE HARD-AND-FAST RULES about the depth of post holes because several factors come into play. In general, the taller the post, the deeper it needs to be sunk in the earth for it to be sturdy. For instance, a 3-ft.-high picket fence post would only need to go down about 1 ft., whereas an 8-ft.-high pergola post would require a hole at least 2 ft. deep.

The type of backfill is also a factor. Hard, dry soil resists movement better than soft, wet soil, so the harder the backfill, the shallower the hole can be. A post that's been set in concrete will be much sturdier than a similar post set in dirt. To see how deep a post hole needs to be,

it's best to experiment. Dig the first hole to a depth of about one quarter the overall length of the post. Set the post, backfill it, and see how it feels. If the post wiggles, pull it out and go deeper. If the post feels rock solid and you've been breaking your back, see if you can get away with a little less depth on the next one.

Unlike structural foundations, garden posts don't need to be set below the frost line. Frost may lift garden posts slightly during the freeze-thaw cycle, but they will settle back down come spring. A few shovelfuls of gravel in the bottom of a hole will help drain water away from the post, minimizing heaving.

An auger mounted on the back of a tractor can dig a large hole in a matter of seconds.

Digging with a two-man powered auger is faster than digging by hand.

cut through the surface roots. You can excavate the first 12 in. or so with a shovel, but beyond that point the sides of the hole will restrict the levering action of the shovel handle, so you'll need to switch to a post-hole digger, sometimes called a clam-shell digger. This tool has a pair of scooping blades attached to long wooden handles. To use it, plunge the digger down into the hole with the handles pressed together. Spread the handles to pinch a scoopful of earth between the blades, then remove the soil and set it to the side of the hole.

In hard soils you'll have to loosen the earth between every few jabs of the post-hole digger, which is when you'll need a bar. Bars are available in many variations, but the most popular style, called a digging bar, has a wide chisel point at one end and a disk-shaped head at the other end (see the drawing on the facing page). The head makes it easier to lift a smooth bar out of a

nurserymen, and fence contractors may have them for hire.

The next step down in hardware is a two-man powered auger (see the photo above). This machine is raised and lowered by hand, and the rotation of the auger is driven by a gas engine. Operating a two-man powered auger is straight-forward in homogenous soils but can be a test of will in rocky ground. When the leading edge of the auger strikes a rock, the considerable force of the machine bounces back at the operators. If you enjoy rototilling, you'll love earth augering. Despite the bone-jarring operation and the noise and fumes of a gas engine, you can get a lot done in a day with one of these machines.

In addition to two-man augers, there are one-man models available. In terms of balance, two persons are much better than one, but one-man augers work well in fine, sandy soil.

Hand tools If you don't want to use machinery of any type, and you want to build up your shoulder muscles, manual post-hole digging is for you. To start, outline the hole with a pointed shovel. If the sod is too thick to pierce with a shovel, a few whacks with a heavy mattock will

Using a "clamshell" post-hole digger is the tried-and-true method of digging post holes. First bring the handles together and jab the earth. Spreading the handles apart will then pinch a scoopful of earth so you can lift it from the hole.

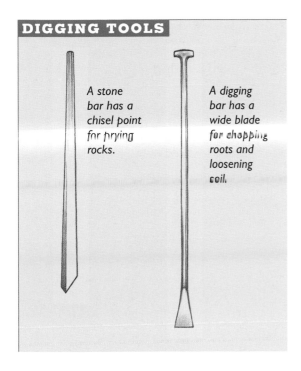

A stone bar has a chisel point for prying rocks.

A digging bar has a wide blade for chopping roots and loosening soil.

hole with sweaty hands and can also be used as a ram for driving rocks during backfilling.

The stone bar is a cousin of the digging bar with a narrow chisel point (see the left drawing above). The stone bar can fit between tightly packed rocks where the wider digging bar cannot reach.

The chisel edge of a bar can easily shear through small roots. Larger roots can be hacked through with the bar, chopped with an ax, or cut with a chainsaw.

Placing the posts

Once the holes are dug, it's time to put in the posts. If pressure-treated timbers are cut up for posts, be sure to put the uncut end of the timber down into the hole. This factory end is more decay resistant than the cut end. To avoid pieces with two cut ends, order appropriate lengths. In other words, for 4-ft. fence posts, order 8-ft. lengths rather than 12-ft. lengths, because a piece taken from the middle of a 12-footer would have no factory end.

Posts are most susceptible to decay at grade level, where both moisture and oxygen are abundant and where the greatest structural stresses on the post occur. For these reasons, when setting tapered cedar or locust poles, place the thicker end of the post in the hole to maximize the amount of wood where it's needed most.

Backfilling

Posts can be set in concrete or simply backfilled with rocks and soil. Concrete obviously costs more but will produce a stronger and more precise installation. Concrete works especially well in marshy places, where water stands in the post hole. In that case, dry concrete is poured around the post. The concrete then cures underwater. When wet concrete is called for, it can be mixed on site by hand or in a drum-type cement mixer. For big jobs, concrete can also be purchased as Redi-Mix®, which is concrete that's mixed in a truck on its way to the site. Whatever type of backfill you use, don't add it all at once; add some, then check that the posts are plumb (straight up and down) before adding more.

Redi-Mix concrete For jobs requiring 1 cu. yd. or more of concrete, the best way to backfill is to order Redi-Mix concrete. You will need an accurate idea of how much concrete is required when you place your order (see the sidebar on p. 38).

Before the Redi-Mix truck arrives, you should carefully consider the scenario for getting concrete from the truck to the post holes. If you're backfilling fence posts along a road, you can simply pour concrete into each hole directly from the truck's chute. More frequently, however, the concrete will need to be poured into wheelbarrows and then distributed to each hole. Have at least one extra helper and wheelbarrow in service for small jobs and a larger crew on hand for quantities of several yards or more.

When using a chainsaw to cut large roots, remove as much dirt from around the root as possible to avoid dulling the chain. Because it's difficult to get dirt out from under a root, don't cut all the way through. Instead, bust through the last inch or so with an ax or bar.

PROTIP

Whenever posts are set in a row, eyeball down the row from one end—any leaners will be easily detected from this vantage point.

Calculating Redi-Mix Concrete Requirements

THE AMOUNT OF CONCRETE BACKFILL required to set a post depends on the size of the post and the size of the hole. Let's take the example of a 4×4 post being set 2 ft. deep in an 8-in.-diameter hole. The volume of the hole is calculated as follows:

$$\pi \times r^2 \text{ (cross sectional area of hole)} \times \text{depth of hole} = \text{volume}$$

which in this case would be:

$$3.14 \times (4 \times 4) \times 24 = 1{,}205 \text{ cu. in.}$$

But part of that volume is taken up by the post, so you need to subtract from this figure the volume of the post below grade, which in this case would be $4 \times 4 \times 24$, or 384 cu. in. The balance is the amount of concrete required, which in this case would be 821 cu. in. The easiest way to convert this number to cubic yards, which is how concrete is ordered, is to divide the balance by 36^3, or 46,656 (the number of cubic inches in a cubic yard). To determine the requirements for hand mixing concrete, see the chart below.

Concrete Requirements

Hole diameter	8 in.	10 in.	12 in.
For 4-in. by 4-in. post			
12 in. deep	36 lb.	65 lb.	101 lb.
18 in. deep	54 lb.	98 lb.	152 lb.
24 in. deep	71 lb.	130 lb.	202 lb.
30 in. deep	89 lb.	163 lb.	253 lb.
For 4-in. round pole			
12 in. deep	39 lb.	69 lb.	105 lb.
18 in. deep	59 lb.	103 lb.	157 lb.
24 in. deep	79 lb.	137 lb.	209 lb.
30 in. deep	98 lb.	172 lb.	262 lb.
For 3-in. round pole			
12 in. deep	45 lb.	74 lb.	110 lb.
18 in. deep	67 lb.	112 lb.	166 lb.
24 in. deep	90 lb.	149 lb.	221 lb.
30 in. deep	112 lb.	186 lb.	276 lb.

Note: To determine the quantity of bags divide by lb./bag (typically 20 lb. or 80 lb.).

TRADE SECRET

If you have a helper, another effective way to mix concrete is to bounce the ingredients up and down on a plastic tarp like a trampoline.

You'll need the extra help because concrete starts hardening as soon as a batch is mixed at the concrete plant, so the quicker it's poured, the less likelihood there will be of the concrete partially setting in the truck. Under no circumstances will a truck driver allow concrete to harden fully in his truck. If you don't get it poured in time, the driver will just pour it out, and you will be the proud owner of a big, gray blob.

To expedite the pour, plan to have enough helpers standing by. Provide easy access for wheelbarrows to each post hole. That means clearing away brush and other obstructions, as well as bridging difficult terrain with planks.

Hand-mixed concrete If the Redi-Mix scenario sounds a little nerve-racking, you can opt for mixing concrete yourself. For small jobs, it's easiest to use a dry concrete premix that contains portland cement, sand, and gravel already mixed in the correct proportions. All you need to do is add water and stir. A bag of premix will typically produce ⅔ cu. ft. of concrete. (See the chart for other premix requirements.)

For larger jobs, it's cheaper—by about 75 percent—to buy sand and gravel in bulk and mix them on site with portland cement. It also ensures that the mix will be fresh. The normal ratio is one part cement to two parts sand and four parts gravel. A sack of cement contains 1 cu. ft., or ¹⁄₂₇ cu. yd., so a typical materials order for 1 cu. yd. of concrete would be 1 cu. yd. of gravel, ½ cu. yd. of sand, and seven sacks (about ¼ cu. yd.) of cement. The volume of concrete produced doesn't equal the combined volume of the ingredients because the sand and cement particles fit in between the gravel stones after mixing.

You'll need to wear eye protection when mixing because concrete is mildly caustic. Concrete can be hand mixed with a shovel or a hoe. It's best to mix on a flat surface such as a sheet of plywood so the ingredients have plenty of room to move around. Once it's mixed, shovel the concrete into a wheelbarrow for transport. Mixing directly in the wheelbarrow saves lifting, but the contours of the wheelbarrow make mixing slower.

The amount of water added to a batch of concrete depends on the dampness of the sand used. If the sand pile is soaked after a rain, no additional water may be necessary. But premix is packaged bone dry, so a fair amount of water must be added. Rather than measure the amount of water, keep an eye on the consistency of the mix. When you pick up a handful and squeeze it,

Concrete for setting posts should be mixed to a stiff consistency.

the concrete should keep its shape but not leave excessive moisture on the palm of your hand (see the photo above). Rinse your hands after performing this test.

For jobs that are too small for ordering Redi Mix but too big to mix by hand, you can rent a cement mixer. Premix can be poured directly into the mixer, whereas bulk ingredients are usually measured in by the shovelful. You will need a hitch on the back of your vehicle to tow the mixer from the rental yard. If you don't have one, most rental yards will fix you up with a hitch at minimal cost.

Soil To backfill a post hole with soil, begin by tossing a stone or two on each side of the post. Pound the stones down tightly around the base of the post. To push the post in one direction or the other, keep adding rocks on the opposite side and drive them in. The post can also be prodded by levering against the side of the hole with a digging bar or a 2×4. When the post is positioned properly in relation to the building line, add a few shovelfuls of soil. Pack the soil in and add some more rocks if you have them. Repeat until the hole is backfilled about halfway.

Check the post with a level to see if it is out of plumb and push it back to plumb if it is. Continue backfilling. Check the post with a level again when the hole is filled, and make any final adjustments by shoving the post and jamming in additional stones just below the surface.

Timber Framing

Heavy timbers are known for earth-retaining projects such as walls and raised beds, but they can also be used for standing structures such as pergolas and bridges when a large scale is called for. This branch of frame construction is known as timber framing. Although the structural principles used in timber framing are the same as for general carpentry, handling and working with heavy timbers requires some special tools and techniques (see the sidebar on the facing page).

The easiest way to cut heavy timbers is with a chainsaw. The chainsaw has a reputation as a rough-cutting monster, but with a little practice you can get surprisingly accurate results. The chain should be sharp and kept properly tensioned. If the chain hangs down more than ⅛ in. below the bottom of the bar, tighten it up. Use a thick carpenter's pencil to lay out a cutline on both the top and side of your timber and line up the bar of the chainsaw much as you would with a handsaw.

Chainsaws also work well for rough notching. First, make the shoulder cuts and the crosscuts in the waste section. Knock out the bulk of the waste with a hammer. To clean up the bottom of the notch, sweep the chainsaw bar carefully from side to side (see the photo below).

To cut timbers more precisely, use a circular saw. A regular 7¼-in. circular saw only cuts about 2½ in. deep, so to complete a crosscut you'll need to cut in from all four sides and then finish the cut with a handsaw. Jumbo circular saws are available that will cut through a 6×6 in a single pass (see the top photo on p. 42). If you have a large project to build, such as a retaining wall, a jumbo saw will speed up your cutting considerably.

You can use a chainsaw to clean up the bottom of a notch by sweeping the cutting bar from side to side.

Moving Timbers Safely

UNSEASONED TIMBERS CAN BE INCREDIBLY HEAVY, so it pays to be careful when moving them. First, to avoid back injury, lift with your knees bent and your back straight. You can alleviate back stress by dragging instead of carrying. Wrap a length of rope around a timber so that two people can carry one end while the other end drags behind. The weight lifted by each person is then only 25 percent of the timber's weight. But it's better to avoid lifting altogether, if possible, so have the timbers dumped off the truck close to the building site. You can also slide timbers along the ground by using small-diameter logs or pipes as rollers.

Overhead lifting is more difficult than simply moving the timbers. To raise a medium-size timber onto posts, begin by bracing the posts securely in both directions. Then set up a sturdy scaffold consisting of sawhorses and heavy planks high enough that a person standing on it will have the tops of the posts about chest high. Lift or slide the timber up on the scaffold, then climb up on the scaffold, and position yourself and your helpers at one end of the timber. First lift one end of the timber onto its post, and hold it in place with scab blocks (short blocks that temporarily straddle the top of the post). Then lift the other end onto its support (see the top photo at right).

Another way to raise a heavy beam is to use skid poles (see the bottom photo at right). These can be square timbers or round poles, but poles actually work better because there will be less contact area (and friction) as a timber slides up the pole. Depending on the height of the lift, timbers can be pushed up the skid poles, pulled with ropes, or both. Pulling with a truck or tractor is also possible.

For large projects, heavy equipment will lift timbers quickly and safely. A backhoe can set beams as high as 12 ft. off the ground, and a small crane, sometimes called a cherry picker, can go even higher.

After lifting one end of the post into place and securing it with scab blocks, set the other end in place.

You can slide a heavy timber into place by pushing it up a pair of skid poles. A board is used here for pushing.

A jumbo circular saw can cut a 6×6 in a single pass.

A bow saw can cut large timbers quickly. Use a block of wood to line up the blade instead of your thumb.

If you have only a few timbers to cut, try a bow saw. This type of handsaw is used mainly for tree pruning, but it works equally well on timbers. A word of caution: When starting a cut with a bow saw, be careful, because the blade of the bow saw is tensioned, causing it to bounce around. Beginners should use a block of wood rather than their thumb to guide the first few strokes of the saw (see the bottom photo at left).

Finishing Techniques

Outdoor finishes are less finicky to apply than their indoor cousins. On the other hand, outdoor finishes need to be renewed much more frequently, so it pays to use the proper tools and techniques.

Careful preparation can make a potentially messy job go smoothly and will produce the best final product. Brushing is the best all-around method for applying finishes, but rolling can speed things up without much extra trouble. For large projects, or those with fussy surfaces such as lattice panels, spraying can save an enormous amount of time.

Preparing the surface

Applying a finish can seem anticlimactic after the excitement of seeing your project take shape, so you may be tempted to slap on a coat of paint and call it a day. But patience and careful preparation are necessary at this stage to produce a finish that is functional, attractive, and durable. Surfaces that will come in contact with human bodies, such as benches, should be sanded to avoid splinters. Sanding also keeps a paint film from cracking at the corners, and a smooth surface provides great moisture resistance. Start with 50-grit paper and finish up with 80 grit. Round all corners and edges slightly.

A random-orbit sander speeds up
a sanding job.

If you have a lot of area to sand, an electric sander will speed things up. The random-orbit type is a good all-around sander that is quick cutting and maneuverable (see the photo above). Belt sanders cut more quickly than random-orbit sanders, but they are clumsier and don't reach into tight spaces as well. Orbital pad sanders are slower than random-orbit sanders. They're used mainly for fine furniture and cabinetry.

Read the label on the can of finish thoroughly to find information on things like proper temperature and compatibility with previous finishes. Stir the contents until all solids are dissolved; stirring takes a long time with stains, which don't dissolve as readily as paint solids. To speed up the process, you can use a paint paddle inserted in an electric drill. The solids in stains and water repellents tend to settle out quickly, so these finishes should be stirred frequently during use.

Brushing

For small- to medium-size projects, brushing remains the simplest and most effective way to apply a finish. Just about all outdoor finishes can be applied with synthetic-bristle brushes (nylon or polyester). For a high-gloss varnish finish, a natural hog-bristle brush will leave fewer brush marks, but the difference is minor. Natural-bristle brushes can also be used for all oil-based finishes but not for water-based finishes—natural bristles absorb water, causing them to go limp.

A 3-in. brush and a 4-in. brush will cover most of your outdoor finishing needs. Because absolute smoothness of finish isn't required in the garden, you won't need a top-of-the-line $15 brush. On the other hand, steer clear of bargain-basement brushes. Not only do they produce poor surface quality, but they also don't hold finish well. As a result, the finish runs all over the place.

For small projects, disposable foam brushes save on cleanup time. These brushes work remarkably well on smooth to semismooth surfaces. They don't work well on rough surfaces, though, because the foam is easily torn.

Begin brushing at the top of your project and work down, brushing out drips and runs as you go. Hold the brush at a slight downward angle whenever possible to keep the finish flowing off the tip, rather than flowing back toward the heel of the brush.

The most demanding brushwork is required by high-gloss enamels. A poor enamel finish will show runs, sags, and coarse brush marks. These flaws don't occur as much when paint-

TRADE SECRET

To protect surrounding surfaces and plantings during finishing, spread drop cloths. Canvas drop cloths are preferable to plastic, because they absorb drips and are limp enough to conform to irregular surfaces.

ing a horizontal surface, because gravity causes the enamel to flow out evenly in all directions. For that reason, it's good to enamel small projects or individual parts in a flat position before they're installed, turning them in phases to dry. The quality of the finish justifies the extra time it takes.

If enameling a vertical surface is unavoidable, keep your brush as dry as possible, working the paint around aggressively. After spreading a thin, even coat over the entire surface, brush it out across the grain. Finally, give the surface a feather-light brushing with the grain. Inspect the surface from different angles to make sure you haven't missed any spots. Inspect the surface again after 15 minutes and brush out any sags that have occurred. If possible, prop a clean sheet of plywood over the work as a temporary roof to protect the finish from airborne debris while it dries.

Spray painting makes short work of outdoor finishing projects. Move the gun parallel to the work to apply an even coat.

Rolling

Rolling is an easy way to speed up a large finishing project such as a pergola. A narrow 4-in. roller works well, and the length of the nap depends on the roughness of the project's surface. Very smooth finish boards require a short nap; regular lumber, including pressure treated, takes a medium-nap roller; and rough-sawn lumber requires a long nap.

When rolling, use long, overlapping strokes. If possible, roll boards in a horizontal position before assembly; paints will flow out better, and stains will have a more even distribution of pigment. If you must work on vertical boards and you need to extend your reach, you can attach a pole handle to the roller.

Stains and water repellents are readily absorbed into a wood surface after being rolled on. However, because paint is somewhat thicker, it should be worked around on the surface a little after rolling to get a good grip. Give it a few vigorous brush strokes right after applying the paint.

Spraying

Spraying is by far the quickest way to apply outdoor finishes (see the photo at left). It's especially time saving on finishing work with lots of nooks and crannies, such as lattice panels. Conventional spray equipment is expensive and tricky to use, but recent advances in spray technology have made spray finishing practical for the homeowner as well as for the professional. Renting equipment makes spraying more economical if you'll need the equipment only once.

Conventional spray rigs consist of a high-pressure air compressor, a hose, and a spray gun. The tip of the gun can be adjusted to produce different spray patterns, depending on the shape of the object being sprayed. A conventional sprayer driven by a gas engine is still the best

An HVLP spray rig is compact and fairly inexpensive

choice for remote projects (such as pasture fences) where electricity is not available.

A new type of sprayer, generically referred to as an HVLP (high-volume low-pressure) sprayer, is the most practical for the do-it-yourselfer, because the equipment is less expensive and more compact (see the photo above). Prices for an HVLP unit start at about $250, whereas a good conventional spray outfit starts at about $500.

A third type of sprayer, called an airless sprayer, is an electric unit that delivers a finish very quickly. This type of sprayer is good for large projects within reach of electricity. An airless sprayer starts at about $400.

Most finishes can be sprayed. Thin finishes, such as water repellent and stain, can be sprayed as is from the can. Heavier finishes, such as oil paints, will spray better if they're thinned down from their normal brushing consistency. However, there is a limit to how much some finishes, such as latex paint, can be thinned, so consult the label. For thick finishes that can be sprayed, guns have interchangeable tips with different-size spray orifices.

After thinning your finish, pour it into the cup of the spray gun through a funnel-shaped filter (available at paint stores). If solid particles enter the gun, they can clog the tip. To strain a heavy finish, you can make your own filter out of insect screen (see the photo below).

Because spraying produces a breathable mist, it is important to use lung protection. Although dust masks are adequate for sanding dust, they don't provide sufficient protection against spray mist—for that you need a respirator with a charcoal filter. When you start smelling finish through the respirator, it's time to change the filter. It's also advisable to wear a stocking cap when spray-painting, to keep finish out of your hair.

Before spraying your project, practice on a few test pieces. Good spray technique depends on maintaining a consistent distance between the spray tip and the workpiece. Start spraying to one side of the work, pass over the work in a straight, steady sweep, and release the trigger after you are beyond the work. If you make a U-turn over the work, you will leave extra material at the edge, which is liable to run.

TRADE SECRET

Some latex paints are not recommended for any spray application whatsoever, so be sure to check the label.

To keep the spray gun from clogging, strain the paint. Use a piece of insect screen as a filter and a milk jug as a funnel.

BORDERS AND STEPS

To garden is to arrange the landscape according to your tastes and necessities. But Mother Nature's concern for these matters is, shall we say, rather low. Plant species stage territorial invasions and counterattacks. Rain washes soil from one place to another. Gravity, that great leveler, joins in the onslaught, shoving your best-laid plans aside with slow, steady purpose.

Wood is one of the most effective weapons in this trench warfare of the garden. In its simplest application, borders can be laid on level ground to define the boundaries between paths, beds, and turf. Borders also help a gardener manage the scheme by clearly defining territory and creating physical barriers to the intermingling of plants. As the grade changes, timbers can be used as steps to make a path more accessible for walking and to control erosion. ▶ ▶ ▶

A border of land-scape timbers separates a bed of tulips from the adjoining lawn.

A railroad-tie border keeps soil from drifting onto the adjoining patio.

The pea gravel covering this path is contained neatly by wooden borders. A filter fabric membrane below the path keeps weeds from infiltrating.

Border Construction

Borders help a gardener to maintain the land-scape by separating diverse elements. For instance, the edge of a lawn can be clearly defined by wood edging (see the left photo above). Without such a barrier, turf must be painstakingly trimmed with a spade. Where slight changes of elevation occur, borders also act as mini retaining walls, preventing the gradual dis-placement of soil from, say, a raised flower bed onto a patio (see the top right photo above).

One of the most important uses of borders is to delineate paths. Although paths can be as informal as a well-worn track through a meadow, hard edging will make a path neater and easier to maintain.

Various pressure–treated products can be used for edging, including square and semisquare timbers. Wide borders such as these are easy to maintain; just run your lawnmower wheel on top of the timber as you mow. For extra-heavy borders, railroad ties work well. You can also use 1×4 boards for thin, almost-invisible borders.

The first step in constructing a border is proper layout. Once location is established, digging a shallow trench will be your next task. In moist, cold climates the trench must then be prepared with filter fabric and gravel to ensure drainage and to prevent frost damage. Then comes the edging itself. If you want to have a path between the borders, you'll need to surface it.

Laying out the border edge

After you've cleared the area, lay out the edge of your border. For straight lines, stretch strings between stakes. For circular curves, first drive a center stake into the ground and then swing a cord with one end tied to the stake. Tie a rebar pin or a stake to the other end of the cord and scratch a curve in the dirt to define your border. You can lay out irregular curves by flexing a thin wooden batten into position between various points and then marking alongside the batten with spray paint or lime.

If you intend to bend your edging into place, use one of the edging boards to lay out the curve so you can be sure your edging material is flexible enough. If your boards are too stiff to take the bend, switch to a thinner board or lay out a gentler curve. You may want a curved border with more thickness so that you can run a mower wheel on top of it. Consider using a wood/polymer product such as Trex bender-board. Wood/polymer is more flexible than regular lumber to begin with, and warming it in the sun will increase its flexibility even further. Instead of bending boards into position, you can approximate a curve with straight timbers.

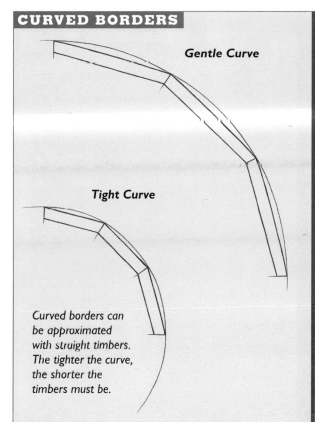

CURVED BORDERS

Gentle Curve

Tight Curve

Curved borders can be approximated with straight timbers. The tighter the curve, the shorter the timbers must be.

The sharper the curve, the shorter the timbers must be (see the drawings above).

Digging and providing drainage

Preparing a straight border is a simple process.
1. Move the stringline over temporarily by about 2 in. This line will establish where to dig. Leave the original stakes in place because you will need to restretch the stringline later on as a guide for setting the edging. Dig a trench along the new stringline location about 4 in. wider than the width of your edging (2 in. on each side) **A** (on p. 50).

2. The depth of the trench depends on your geographical location. You'll need to dig to a depth about equal to the thickness of the border timber. In addition, in frost-prone regions edging should be laid on a bed of compacted

PRO TIP

If you want a curved border, use thin boards. They are flexible, allowing them to conform to gentle curves.

gravel to promote drainage, so you'll need to dig deeper to allow for 2 in. to 3 in. of gravel below the edging **B**. When edging is laid directly on dirt, it can be adversely affected by frost heaving (see the sidebar on the facing page). In tropical environments, gravel can be omitted below the edging, but it's still advisable to overdig the trench about 1 in. to allow for a setting bed of compacted sand. The sand makes it easy to level the timbers.

3. When preparing a path, remove grass and soil from between the border trenches as well so that the surface of the path finishes out at the desired height. Stripping topsoil also removes the roots of perennial weeds. Some landscapers recommend the application of an herbicide at this point as well.

Putting down filter fabric

Synthetic filter fabric acts as a root barrier, yet allows water to pass through for good drainage. Without filter fabric, topsoil washes into the gravel bed below the edging and prevents the gravel from drawing water away from the edging.

1. After digging your trench, lay in strips of synthetic filter fabric. The fabric should extend about 6 in. beyond the outside of the trench (it will be folded tight against the edging later on).

In the case of a path, fabric should also extend between the two border trenches to discourage the roots of annual weeds from finding moisture in the subsoil below the path. Depending on the width of the path, you may be able to line the path and the trenches with a single wide strip of fabric.

2. After lining the trench, fill it with clean, coarse gravel. Level the gravel with a straight-

Dealing with Frost Heaving

FROST HEAVING OCCURS DURING LATE FALL and early spring when soggy soil freezes and thaws. Freezing causes the soil to expand, thus lifting anything on top of the soil, whether it is a single 4×4 or an entire building. When the ground thaws, the soil settles back down.

If everything were to rise and fall evenly, there would not be a problem. But soil in one spot often lifts more than that in another spot just a few feet away. Expansion may vary from side to side as well, with the soil expanding outward as well as upward. As objects on top of the soil get bumped around by this uneven expansion, the wet soil beneath them slumps and shifts. As a result, the wooden border that lined up straight as an arrow last fall may appear lumpy and crooked come spring.

To completely avoid frost heaving, structures must extend below the frost line—the depth at which the ground never freezes. (The frost line varies from a few inches below grade in the Deep South to 4 ft. or more in the northern United States and Canada.) Most informal garden structures can tolerate a little uneven-ness without spoiling their looks, so digging below frost isn't always necessary. Instead, you can place gravel between the structure and the soil to drain water away from the structure. Any water that remains in or around the gravel is free to expand into the spaces between the gravel stones as freezing occurs.

edge as shown in **C** and tamp it down with a 4×4 or the end of a sledgehammer.

Installing the edging

Digging and prepping your trenches with gravel is the most arduous part of a border or path. In comparison, laying the edging itself goes quickly. To guide the installation, you'll need to restretch your stringlines. These lines will guide the exact placement of your timbers or boards. The way you fasten the edging will depend on whether you are using timber or board edging. After installing the edging, you'll fill on both sides to complete the job.

Timber edging The following steps will lead you to a good-looking and long-lasting border.

1. Reset the stringlines and lay your timbers to the line. Keep the straightest side of each timber on edge for appearance's sake, because

Using a high-grade material such as cedar for the cover boards hides defects in the rougher-grade timbers below.

TIMBER EDGING

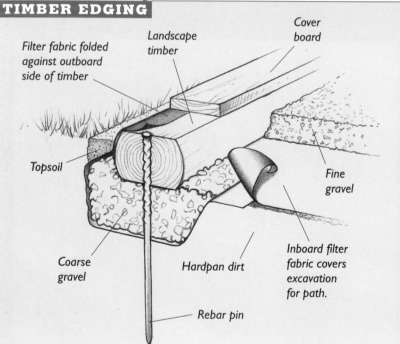

Filter fabric folded against outboard side of timber

Landscape timber

Cover board

Topsoil

Fine gravel

Coarse gravel

Hardpan dirt

Inboard filter fabric covers excavation for path.

Rebar pin

warped edges are especially noticeable as they're approached along a straight path.

2. Now pin the timbers in place with lengths of rebar or 12-in. spikes (see the drawing at left). Drill clearance holes in the timbers so that the rebar penetrates easily. Drive the pins in place with a sledgehammer, as shown in **D**, then inspect the border by eyeballing it from one end. If any of the timbers have been knocked sideways, tap them back into position with the sledgehammer.

3. When installing a border with dirt on both sides, such as between a lawn and a flower bed, fold the filter fabric against the timber on both sides. If the border has a gravel bed on one side, however, simply overlap the border fabric with the fabric under the gravel bed. Hold the fabric in place on the dirt side (or sides) by adding backfill. After tamping the backfill, trim off the excess fabric with a knife an inch or so above grade level.

4. Now splice the ends of the edging timbers. You can fasten metal truss plates to the sides of adjoining timbers, toenail them together, or use a half-lap splice (for more on joinery options, see p. 28).

E

TRADE SECRET

Bark is especially appropriate for woodland settings, whereas marble chips produce a bright white surface that can really set off adjacent colors. For paths leading directly into the house, use a washed gravel to avoid tracking in dust.

Another way to splice the edging timbers and hold them in alignment is to use cover boards (thin, flat boards placed on top of the edging timbers). If you use cover boards, fold the fabric over the top of the timber and staple it in place before capping to provide an extra measure of protection against weeds, as shown in **E**. For strength, offset the joints in the cover boards from the joints in the edging timbers by at least 2 ft. Attach the cover boards with galvanized nails or screws, as shown in **F**. Pre-drill the cover boards so they won't split.

5. Fill the path with pea gravel, or whatever surface material you've chosen.

6. Spread and level the gravel with an iron rake, as shown in **G**, then compact it with a tamper. Finally, backfill against the outsides of the timbers with topsoil.

F

G

Brick Path Edged with Timber

IN FORMAL SETTINGS, A BRICK PATH is attractive. To accommodate bricks, excavate the entire path to the same depth as the border trenches. This will leave room for a bed of stone dust on which to lay the bricks.

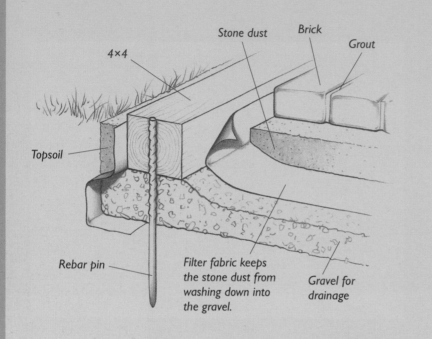

4×4

Stone dust

Brick

Grout

Topsoil

Rebar pin

Filter fabric keeps the stone dust from washing down into the gravel.

Gravel for drainage

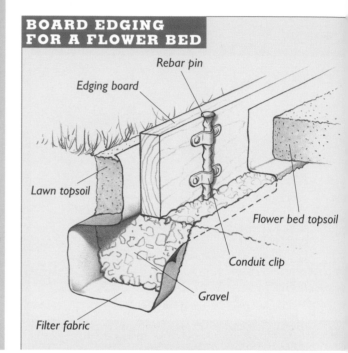

BOARD EDGING FOR A FLOWER BED

Rebar pin

Edging board

Lawn topsoil

Flower bed topsoil

Conduit clip

Gravel

Filter fabric

Thin boards create a low-profile edging for this flower bed. The boards are fastened to rebar pins with galvanized conduit clips.

Board edging Board edging can be fastened to 1×2 wooden stakes or rebar pins (see the right drawing on the facing page). Keep the stakes or pins on the least-conspicuous side. For instance, when building a typical flower bed/turf border, put your stakes on the flower-bed side, where they can be hidden by mulch. In the case of stakes, drive outdoor screws through the edging into the stake once the stake is in place.

When using rebar pins, fasten them to edging with galvanized conduit clips (see the photo and the right drawing on the facing page). The clips are sold in different sizes for attaching electrical conduit. The nominal ½-in. size works well with a ⅝-in. rebar pin.

Filter fabric interfaces with board edging in the same way it does with timber edging. As for splicing and alignment, board edging is too thin to be capped with a cover board, but you can splice the boards with a thin metal "truss plate" nailed to the vertical sides of the boards. The plate won't be visible after backfilling.

Step Construction

Garden steps can be built quickly and relatively cheaply with railroad ties or PT timbers (see the photo above right). The thickness of a railroad tie (7 in.) is very near to the ideal riser height (vertical dimension) used for house steps. So are the dimensions of 8×8 PT timbers, whose actual dimensions run between 7 in. and 8 in. (depending on whether or not they're planed). Surfaced 6×6s, which actually measure 5½ in. square, make for a rather low step, but this may actually suit the pace of a leisurely garden stroll.

With such amenable materials at hand, building landscape steps isn't terribly difficult. The key is spending some time on a well thought out design.

Heavy timbers are useful for creating steps. These woodland steps are made with pressure-treated timbers, which are lighter in color and weigh less than railroad ties.

Steps that follow the slope

A straight stepped path, say across a lawn and down to a pond, is the simplest to build.

1. Begin by laying out the path with stakes and stringlines.

2. Starting at the bottom of the path, set the first riser (cross timber) in a shallow bed of compacted gravel. Cut half-lap joints on the ends of this first riser to accept mating half laps on the first pair of stringers (side timbers). Succeeding steps won't require half laps because both riser and stringer have a step below to which they can be spiked (see the drawing on p. 56).

3. Butt one end of each stringer into a riser in front, with the other end buried into the slope. The stringer must extend back far enough to provide a solid foundation for the next riser. To determine this, set one end of a level on the first riser and move the other end of the level up or down the slope until the bubble reads

PRO TIP

Make stakes for board edging from PT yellow pine, even when using cedar or redwood for the edging, because yellow pine holds screws more tenaciously than cedar or redwood and stands up better under the blows of a sledgehammer.

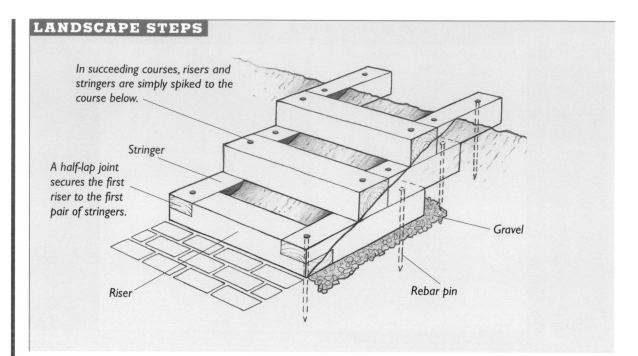

LANDSCAPE STEPS

In succeeding courses, risers and stringers are simply spiked to the course below.

Stringer

A half-lap joint secures the first riser to the first pair of stringers.

Gravel

Riser

Rebar pin

PRO TIP

If you live in a frost-prone region and you want to prevent all threats of frost heaving, overdig all of the trenches, add gravel, and lay all the stringers on top of the gravel.

true (centered in the vial). This is about where the front of the next riser will be located. Dig past this point at least another foot and lay a few inches of gravel in the trench.

4. Set the first stringers in place and drill through the half-lap joints at each end. Drive 2-ft. lengths of rebar through the joints and down into the ground. Pin the opposite (soon to be buried) ends to the earth also.

5. Then lay the second riser across the stringers and spike it in position.

6. Use the level to determine how deep the next pair of side trenches should extend (see the drawing on the facing page). Scrape these trenches level with the top surfaces of the preceding stringers before you install the stringers. This will keep the stringers level with the previous steps. If you overdig, build the bottom of the trench back up with gravel or compacted earth.

7. After spiking the second pair of stringers to the first pair (and to the slope), set the third riser. Continue in this fashion until you reach the top of the path. The treads should all be the same width so that people won't trip (there's more on determining tread width in the next section).

8. Backfill the completed stairs with earth or a hard-packing aggregate such as crusher run. The surface of the steps can also be paved with cobbles or cordwood pavers (2-in.-thick wooden disks crosscut from the end of a log). Or use brick infill for a formal effect (see the photo on the facing page).

Steps for difficult slopes

The slope of most garden landscapes is lower than the ideal stair pitch of 7:10. Although the rules for indoor stairs are quite strict, the rules for outdoor stairs are more flexible because people are more careful when stepping outside.

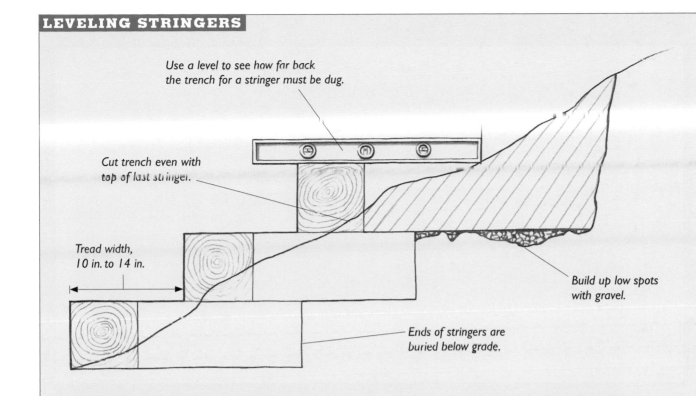

Use a level to see how far back the trench for a stringer must be dug.

Cut trench even with top of last stringer.

Tread width, 10 in. to 14 in.

Build up low spots with gravel.

Ends of stringers are buried below grade.

These steps are paved with brick and edged with 6×6s. The tread surfaces are pitched downhill for good drainage. The brick pattern is called basket weave.

Defining Pitch

THE PRINCIPLES GOVERNING THE DESIGN of house stairs also apply to landscape stairs. In either case, the steepness of a staircase is expressed as pitch, which is the ratio of the stair's overall height to its overall width (see the drawings at right). For instance, a staircase might rise 7 ft. vertically between the bottom step and the top step while traversing a horizontal distance of 10 ft. Each individual step would be a sort of microcosm of the entire staircase, having a riser height of 7 in. and a tread width (horizontal dimension) of 10 in. In both cases, the pitch is expressed as the ratio 7:10.

Stairs that are too steep are exhausting to climb and dangerous to descend. On the other hand, stairs that rise too slowly can be tedious, requiring an awkward shuffle. The optimum pitch for stairs is about 7:10. Accordingly, a straight set of landscape steps imposed on a hillside with a 7:10 pitch would be comfortable to climb. In the natural world, of course, hillsides with 7:10 pitch are the exceptions rather than the rule, so you may have to build your stairs on a difficult slope.

Pitch is a way of measuring slope, expressed as the ratio of vertical rise to horizontal travel. All three of the conditions below have a 7:10 pitch.

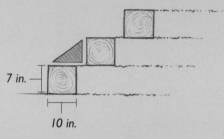

The ratio of a 7-in. stair riser to a 10-in. stair tread

7 in.

10 in.

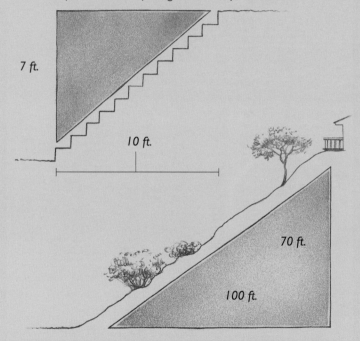

The ratio of a staircase's 7-ft. height to its 10-ft. breadth

7 ft.

10 ft.

70 ft.

100 ft.

The ratio of a hillside's 70-ft. height to its 100-ft. breadth

That means you can deviate from the 7:10 standard to accommodate a gently rising slope. A riser/tread ratio as low as 7:14 would be acceptable in the garden. Don't make the tread less than 10 in. wide, or people will be likely to trip. On the other hand, an excessively wide tread should be avoided.

As the width of the tread increases, the stride of the person using the stairs gets stretched as well. For slopes lower than 7:14, it's better to build up the stairway into level terraces connected by two or three standard 7:10 steps (see the drawing on the facing page). The term "terrace" in this case means an extrawide step, similar

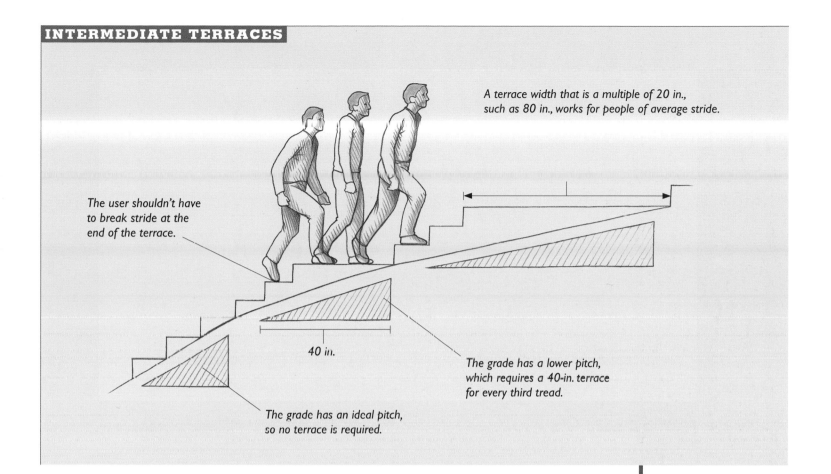

A terrace width that is a multiple of 20 in., such as 80 in., works for people of average stride.

The user shouldn't have to break stride at the end of the terrace.

40 in.

The grade has a lower pitch, which requires a 40-in. terrace for every third tread.

The grade has an ideal pitch, so no terrace is required.

to the term "landing" as applied to interior staircases. The construction of the terraces is the same as for standard treads, except that the stringers are longer. The length of each terrace should be close to a multiple of 20 in. (i.e., 20 in., 40 in., 60 in.), which will locate the next riser in a convenient location for the average person. It's annoying and dangerous to have to shorten or lengthen one's stride as a riser approaches, especially with a bag of groceries under each arm. If you're exceptionally short or tall, you may want to mock up the length of a proposed terrace to see how it works with your stride. If the slope of the hillside changes over the course of the stairs, add or subtract risers as needed to lengthen or shorten the next terrace.

Although slopes that are too gentle can be terraced upward without too much difficulty,

hillsides that are too steep present a tougher problem. One way to build a comfortable stair here is to cut into the hillside. At that point, something must be done to keep the sides of the cut from collapsing. If heavy equipment is available, the easiest solution may be to slope back the sides of the cut to the point where plantings will hold the soil in place. Landscapers call this the "angle of repose," and it varies depending on soil type and what type of groundcover you intend to use. Certain shrubs, for instance, will tolerate a steeper angle than grass. A qualified excavator will know how steep to grade the cut.

Another option for a steep site would be to build a pair of timber flank walls alongside the staircase (see pp. 68–73). Timber risers can be easily woven into these flank walls to produce a staircase. Timber walls are dealt with in Chapter 5.

TRADE SECRET

Intermittent terraces in a set of steps do more than just create an acceptable stair pitch. They also give the user a breather between flights of steps, in the same way that an intermediate landing does with an interior staircase.

DESIGN
OPTIONS

▲ **This perennial bed has been edged with short redwood timbers set vertically into the ground. Staggering the tops of the timbers rather than setting them even imparts a naturalistic feel.**

◀ Pressure-treated
8×8s have been
stacked to make
a set of steps.
The low-voltage
light fastened to
the lowermost
rIser illuminates
the path in the
foreground.

◀ The precise
regularity of a
brick border fits
nicely with the
geometric layout of
this formal garden.

▲ A set of steps
made of 2×6 boards
nailed together is
an easy and eco-
nomical solution.

◀ Edging with gran-
ite blocks set flush
with the adjoining
turf makes an easy-
to-care-for border.
It can be main-
tained simply by
mowing over it.

RETAINING WALLS

To make a hillside stable and accessible, it can be terraced with a series of wood retaining walls. To design a terraced landscape, you'll need to determine the number, height, and configuration of the terrace(s). Environmental factors, such as exposure to wind and sun, as well as practical requirements, such as the need for building space, must also be taken into account. The job's level of difficulty will be affected by your decisions. A retaining wall of any kind involves the moving of a lot of heavy stuff, so it pays to consider all the design options up front.

As for the actual building of wood retaining walls, there's literally more to it than meets the eye. That's because buried timbers are used to anchor retaining walls to the earth behind them. This anchoring enables a wall to withstand the tremendous pressure generated by wet or frozen earth. To keep this pressure to a minimum, proper drainage is essential. ▶ ▶ ▶

Retaining Wall Design

You'll have to address two major issues when you design a retaining wall. One is the size of the terrace created adjacent to the wall. The second is the wall's relationship to the hillside on which it stands. A wall can be fully recessed into a hill, built entirely on top of it, or a combination of both.

TERRACE SIZE

Terrace size will be determined by the height of the adjacent retaining wall. The taller the wall, the larger the terrace.

One Large Terrace

Intermittent Terraces

Low Steps

Terrace size

The size and number of terraces is the designer's first decision (see the drawing at left). At one extreme, you can wall off an entire slope, creating a single large terrace. A large terrace may be more useful than several smaller ones, especially when a major feature such as a patio or an outbuilding must be accommodated. On lots that are steeply sloped, tall retaining walls may be the only way to create necessary space.

The problem with creating one large terrace is that it maximizes the building effort involved. As the height of a wall increases, the loads it must withstand also increase (see the sidebar below). Consequently, the wall must be not only bigger but also stronger, which means using heavier timbers, larger fasteners, and more tiebacks (anchoring timbers).

A single large terrace also requires a lot more digging or filling than a succession of smaller ones, so heavy equipment is almost certainly necessary. Because of these construction challenges, retaining walls over 5 ft. tall are best left to licensed, insured contractors and should never be attempted without first consulting a structural engineer.

Instead of one big terrace, you can sculpt a slope into a series of smaller terraces (see the photo on the facing page). The width of each

Ground Forces

RETAINING WALLS MUST WITHSTAND terrific pressure from the earth they hold back. Although dry soil exerts a lot of weight, to some extent a pile of dry earth is self supporting. On the other hand, when soil is saturated with water it becomes semiliquid. That's when the real test begins.

To grasp the problem, think of a bag of rice. In its dry state, the rice can easily be contained in a thin plastic bag. But if you soak that rice in water, it becomes heavier, and the water acts as a lubricant so that the grains of rice slide more easily against each other. After a while, the rice starts to swell and the bag finally bursts. Multiply this scenario a few thousand times, and you get some idea of the pressure acting on a retaining wall after a rainstorm.

In the winter, the problem worsens. As wet ground freezes, ice causes the soil to expand even more. Once a retaining wall is kicked outward by frozen ground, it stays that way; as temperatures rise, thawed-out soil settles into the wedge-shaped void left between the earth and the back of the wall. There's only one way to repair this: reconstruct the wall.

A series of low retaining walls has been used to [.......] this steep site. Boulders have been incorporated into the lowermost course to achieve a natural look.

terrace should provide for a comfortable path, as well as for any planting beds that are desired. This scheme looks more natural than one large, overbearing grade change and requires less work. If the grade isn't too steep and you don't need too wide an area, a series of low walls is your best bet.

To keep the look even more natural, you can terrace a gentle slope to create actual steps, with each "retaining wall" consisting of a single timber. This technique stabilizes a slope with a minimum of effort. However, the width of the resulting terraces may be too narrow for practical purposes, especially on a steep grade.

Digging options

The second decision in retaining-wall design is whether to cut into a bank, add fill on top of it, or do a combination of both (see the drawing on p. 66). Cutting into a bank completely means that the resulting terrace is fully recessed below the surface of the hillside. Retaining walls will be required to hold back the remaining earth at the back and sides of the terrace. The opposite approach is to build a retaining wall above grade and then fill in behind it. A middle course is to cut away part of the bank, build a wall at the back of the cut, and then use the removed dirt to fill in behind an above-grade wall on the downhill side.

Recessed terrace A fully recessed terrace has an enclosed, intimate feeling similar to a courtyard garden in town. Because the terrace consists of recessed wing walls flanking a main wall in back, the view from the terrace is directed to the front, which could be an advantage or a disadvantage, depending on local scenery. As with city gardens, the choice of plants here may be affected by a limited exposure to sunlight, and of course you must consider what to do with all the fill dirt generated by digging this type of terrace.

Built-up terrace To create a built-up terrace, you can build your retaining wall entirely on top

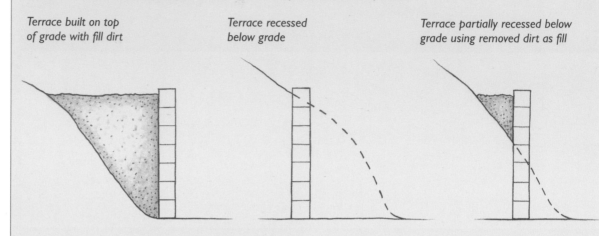

CUT, FILL, OR BOTH?

Terraces can be built on top of grade, below grade, or by a combination of both.

Terrace built on top of grade with fill dirt

Terrace recessed below grade

Terrace partially recessed below grade using removed dirt as fill

This tall retaining wall has been back-filled to create a broad terrace. Notice the tubing installed at the base of the wall to provide drainage.

of the existing grade and fill in behind it, provided that you have enough fill dirt and an access road to get it to your wall location. A built-up terrace has a raised, airy feeling. The view is extended on all sides, and the area receives lots of sunlight. Welcome breezes are found here in summer, but so are chill winds in autumn and spring.

Cut and filled terrace To avoid importing or exporting fill dirt, you can recess your retaining wall halfway into a bank and use the excavated dirt and rock to fill in behind the wall. If you have no way to bring in trucks or digging equipment to the site, this is the most practical option.

Retaining Wall Construction

Pressure-treated timbers (6×6 or 8×8), railroad ties, and semisquare landscape timbers are commonly used for retaining walls. Square PT timbers create the cleanest, most geometric look. Railroad ties have a rougher appearance, and their dark color helps them recede into the background. Semisquare landscape timbers have the most texture of the three, as well as a rustic, backwoods connotation.

Masonry walls rely largely on their own weight to resist the pressure of the soil behind them, but wood retaining walls are lighter, so they must be anchored to the adjoining earth. If a wall isn't anchored, it will lean and bulge.

Retaining walls turn a sloped site into a succession of level terraces. The wall on the right is made of railroad ties. The wall on the left is made of pressure-treated timbers.

Installing tiebacks

To anchor wood retaining walls effectively, use buried timbers, called tiebacks. Tiebacks run roughly perpendicular to the face of the wall and are placed every 8 ft. or so. Tiebacks should reach back far enough to provide plenty of soil weight on top of them, and should be positioned deep in the lower courses, rather than just below the surface, for the same reason. There are several ways to secure tiebacks into a slope, and the methods can be used separately or in combination with each other (see the drawings at right).

The first method is to pin tiebacks into undisturbed soil using 2-ft. lengths of reinforcing bar (called rebar). This method is effective as long as the soil is hard enough and the tiebacks reach back far enough. For a more secure way to anchor a wood retaining wall, create a strong framework, called a crib, behind the exposed wall. At the back of the crib, stack cross ties between the tiebacks in log-cabin fashion. When the crib is buried with gravel and dirt, the weight of the backfill supports the wall.

For a more economical alternative to the full-crib design, spike short blocks to the ends of individual tiebacks. The resulting "T" configuration works like a ship's anchor to hook each tieback into the embankment.

ANCHORING RETAINING WALLS

Tiebacks can be pinned directly to the slope or interwoven with cross ties to form a crib. Backfill holds the crib in place. In lieu of a crib, short T-blocks can be used to anchor the cross ties.

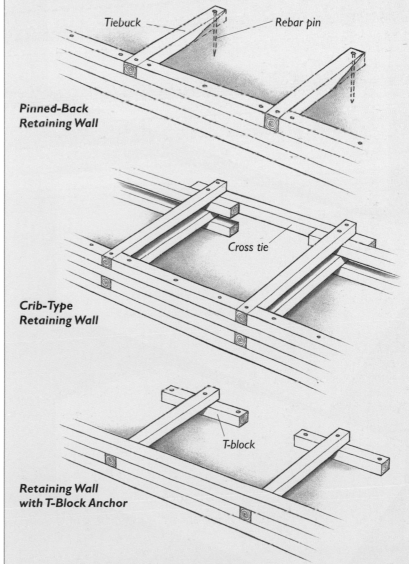

Tieback — Rebar pin

Pinned-Back Retaining Wall

Cross tie

Crib-Type Retaining Wall

T-block

Retaining Wall with T-Block Anchor

Fastening Wood with Rebar

GALVANIZED SPIKES CAN BE USED TO fasten timbers if they're at least 1½ times as long as the timber is thick. If spikes aren't available, however, you can use lengths of concrete reinforcing bar (rebar). Rebar can also be used to pin timbers to the earth, such as for borders and retaining walls. Rebar is typically sold in 20-ft. lengths, but precut lengths of 12 in., 18 in., and 24 in. may be available. For corrosion resistance, use galvanized or plastic-coated rebar. Some suppliers will custom-cut rebar for you on a special shear or with an oxy-acetylene torch.

If you need to cut rebar on the job site, use a hacksaw or an abrasive metal-cutting blade mounted in a circular saw. After cutting about three-quarters of the way through, bend the bar back and forth to snap the piece in two.

You don't need to form a point on the end of a rebar "pin," as long as you drill a clearance hole through both timbers. A head on one end is also unnecessary because the rough surface of rebar pins causes them to hold well.

Use a circular saw equipped with an abrasive wheel to cut rebar.

BATTERING A TIMBER RETAINING WALL

Timbers are stacked with a slight offset, called battering, to increase the wall's strength. Gravel, drainpipe, and filter fabric ensure good drainage.

Filter fabric

Compacted fill

Soil

Battering

Perforated drain

Battering

To alleviate pressure at the top of the wall, it helps to "batter" the wall's face by offsetting each course of timbers by ¾ in. to produce a backward tilt (see the left photo on the facing page). The resulting flare at the bottom of the wall has a buttressing effect, helping to support the earth behind the wall. Besides being stronger, a battered wall has a more solid look than a wall with a truly vertical face. Also, offsetting the timbers lends a texture to the wall's finished surface.

Building a Wall with Steps

Compared to masonry walls, timber walls such as this one are quick and inexpensive. It's not difficult to build stairs at the same time as you build the wall to provide access to the level above the wall (see the top right photo on the facing

This retaining wall forms a bed for colorful plantings.

Battering gives this timber retaining wall texture and a solid look. A blue-gray stain helps the wall blend into its surroundings.

page). A six-course wall is about as high as you would typically build on your own. Higher walls encounter greater soil pressures and require lots of heavy earth moving, so you'd probably need to hire a professional for the job.

1. Dig the trenches for the main wall and the wing wall(s), as shown in **A**. Burying the foot of the wall is critical so the wall won't slide forward under pressure. The trenches should be about three times the width of the timbers, and three times as deep.

2. Line the trenches with filter fabric. Place a 2-in.-thick layer of gravel on the bottom of the trenches. Use a clean, coarse crushed stone such as #57 (#57 is stone-yard terminology for gravel stones about 1 in. long).

On the bottom of the trench place a perforated plastic drainage tube and surround it with gravel. Be sure to specify perforated tubing because a solid-wall variety is also available. The

A

B

C

D

3. Lay the first course (or layer) of timber in the gravel bed below grade. Use a 4-ft. spirit level to check that the timber is level before you proceed. If not, adjust the gravel bed and try again, as shown in **C**.

4. To keep the first course from sliding forward, place well-compacted backfill against it on the outside of the wall, as shown in **D**. It should finish flush with the top of the base course of timber.

A buffer of filter fabric and a 1-ft. wall of gravel should come between the back of the wall and any soil. As water seeps out of the soil into the gravel buffer, it runs down between the stones, finding its way to the perforated drain. With this drainage, the hydrostatic pressure behind the wall never builds up to the danger level.

drainage tube must extend to some convenient drop-off point, such as a dry well, an underground storm drain, or daylight (any point at grade level downhill from the wall). Local building codes prohibit the emptying of groundwater into sanitary sewers. When laying the drain, be sure that its holes face down **B**; otherwise, large dirt particles and other trash could enter the drain, causing it to clog. Then cover the tubing with gravel.

5. To determine the extent of the cut for the first stair stringer, place a scrap of timber on the base course. With the scrap to simulate the stringer, use a level to carry the height of the stringer over to the hillside. Mark the far end of the cut with spray paint, as shown in **E**.

6. Dig a trench for the stringer and place gravel in the bottom so the top of the gravel bed is flush with the top of the base course of timbers. Then place the stringer in the trench and mark its length for cutting, as shown in **F**, or take a measurement to cut the stringer. This is the same process to follow for all succeeding stringers. Install another stringer in the first course to flank the stair, and cut the risers in the front of the wall to fit to fit between the stringers.

7. Spike the stringers and risers to the base course with rebar, as shown in **G**.

8. Spike the second riser to a stringer, as shown in **H**. This stringer will become a part of the flank wall, which terminates the retaining wall. Continue on with the rest of the courses in the same way.

9. Use a framing square in conjunction with a level to lay out the digging for the first tie-back, as shown in **I**. Cut pockets into the slope

The End of the Wall

HOW A RETAINING WALL TERMINATES depends on its relationship to the adjoining hillside (see the drawings below). If the wall cuts all the way across a hill, its ends will simply taper down to grade in succeeding courses. With a terrace recessed into a hillside, the wing walls step down to grade in similar fashion, whereas the main wall is interlocked with the wing walls in log-cabin fashion. When a terrace is built out from a hillside, the wing-wall timbers step up rather than down, with their ends buried into the slope. The installation in this last case is similar to burying stair stringers (see p. 56). Pin each course in the wing wall to the slope with rebar, and tie any buried cribbing into the wing walls as well for strength.

TERMINATIONS FOR RETAINING WALLS

Retaining walls can be terminated in different ways, depending on the surrounding topography.

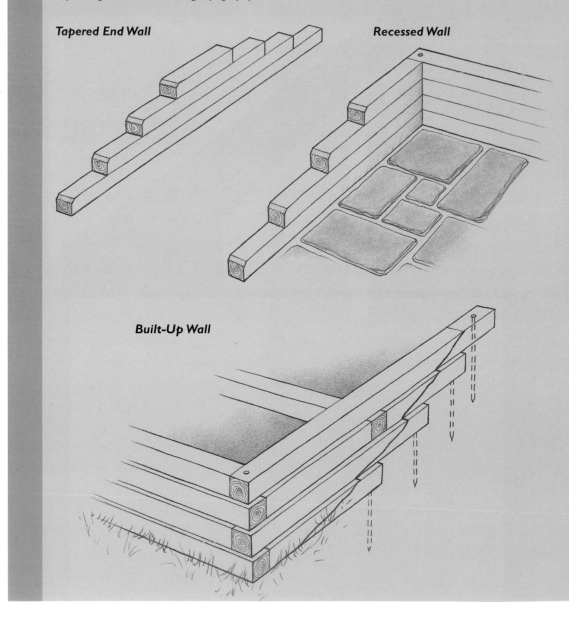

Tapered End Wall

Recessed Wall

Built-Up Wall

to receive the buried end of each tieback and spike the tiebacks to the wall in front and to the earth in back with rebar, as shown in **J**.

10. The next course consists of more wall timbers in front and cross ties or T-blocks in back. Fasten cross ties to the buried ends of the tiebacks in the preceding course, as shown in **K**. Instead of splicing cross ties end to end on the tieback, stagger them so that both timbers get a good purchase on the tieback (see the drawing on p. 67). Use the same alternating pattern until you reach the second-to-last course, when you no longer need to use tiebacks. Once the timber work is complete, as shown in **L**, pour in the gravel backfill. You can fill the steps in with the same materials you would use for paths.

DESIGN
OPTIONS

▼ A retaining wall of pressure-treated timbers is quick and easy to install compared to a masonry wall. Stairs have been integrated with this wall to make the slope accessible.

◀ Modular concrete blocks are permanent and fairly easy to install. In this example, a mix of different sizes helps to soften the factory-made look characteristic of these products.

◀ Round-edged landscape timbers have been stacked here to build up a level terrace for a prefabricated play structure.

◀ A low retaining wall of unpeeled cedar logs is used here to stabilize a steep site. Also note the use of vertical saplings as piling at the water's edge.

RAISED BEDS

A raised bed filled with enriched soil can produce a bountiful harvest in a small footprint and can add an interesting vertical dimension to an otherwise flat site. A raised bed is also easy to cultivate because you don't have to bend over far to rake soil or to pull weeds. What's more, a raised bed provides excellent drainage, even when filled with heavy soil.

Raised beds can be built from many different types of lumber. They also employ different methods for countering the pressure generated by contained soil. Soil pressure can cause a raised bed to bulge in the middle, or, worse yet, to split apart at the corners. One type of raised bed uses stakes to resist soil pressure. Other types depend on wood or metal cross ties to hold them together in the middle. ▶ ▶ ▶

Designing a Raised Bed

The gardener's reach should determine the width of a raised bed. The standard width is 4 ft. to 5 ft., which requires a 2-ft. to 2½-ft. reach from both sides. A bed narrower than this won't provide much tillable area after deducting the thickness of the bed's sides. The bed can be as long as you like, provided you use enough stakes or cross ties to keep the sides from spreading (see the chart below). If you don't want any stakes or cross ties, the length of the bed will be limited by the strength of the sides.

The height of the bed will be a compromise between an aching back, which calls for a higher bed, and outward-thrusting soil pressure, which increases as the height of a bed rises. Also, filling even a small bed with dirt is a big job, especially if you have to dig it up from somewhere else. An ample raised-bed height would be 15 in. to 19 in., requiring a pair of 2×8s or a pair of 2×10s, respectively, as side boards. Lower beds made from a single 2×12 also work well, as long as the soil placed in the bed is complemented by friable native soil below.

Although nominal 2-in.-thick pressure-treated lumber is the most common material for a raised bed, you can use other thicknesses as well. Thinner materials such as 5/4×6 (pronounced five-quarter by six) will require more stakes or cross ties to compensate for the reduction in strength compared to 2× lumber. Nominal 1-in. lumber, which is actually only ¾ in. thick, isn't really strong enough for a raised bed.

These raised beds are constructed of 4×6s with log-cabin corners. The heavy sides resist bowing out.

Spacing Stakes or Cross Ties for Raised Bed

Nominal thickness of side boards	Actual thickness of side boards	Spacing of intermediate stakes or cross ties*	
		PT yellow pine PT douglas fir	Redwood, cedar, or cypress
5/4x	1 in.	3 ft.	2 ft.
2x	1½ in.	4 ft.	3 ft.
4x	3½ in.	8 ft.	6 ft.
6x	5½ in.	12 ft.	10 ft.

*This is also the maximum length of the raised bed if no intermediate supports are used.

This vertical timber bed provides an oasis in the middle of a paved courtyard.

These raised beds of pressure-treated lumber have hoops for removable cloches.

Pressure-Treated Lumber in Raised Beds

PRESSURE-TREATED LUMBER SEEMS like the ideal material for a raised bed. Not only is it guaranteed against rot, but the species most widely treated, southern yellow pine, has the strength needed to withstand soil pressures. If you're growing edible plants, however, you need to consider soil contamination.

PT lumber contains copper, a heavy metal. In theory, leaching of the copper compounds used in PT lumber should not occur, because the compounds are bound to the wood's cell structure as an "insoluble metal complex." On the other hand, nobody claims that PT lumber will last forever, so what happens in 20, 30, or 40 years, when the stuff finally starts to rot? One of the leading treatment manufacturers cautions against using treated wood in areas where you are growing food or animal feed. So, for peace of mind, use a naturally decay-resistant wood, such as construction-grade redwood, when building a raised vegetable bed, even if its life span is limited to 10 or 15 years.

If you're planting edibles, avoid PT lumber and landscape timbers and instead build your raised bed from a naturally decay-resistant species, such as redwood, cedar, or cypress (for more on the safety of PT lumber, see the sidebar at right). These woods aren't as strong as yellow pine or Douglas fir, the two most commonly treated species, so you'll need to place stakes or cross ties closer together.

If there's a sawmill nearby, look into the possibility of using a decay-resistant species of fresh-cut lumber. There's no point in buying seasoned lumber for a raised bed, where ground moisture will always be present.

Laying Out and Preparing the Site

A raised bed that will be placed on a patio or driveway has a ready-made foundation. It can be assembled on site, shoved into position, and filled. A raised bed on a deck or rooftop should

Landscape timbers have a flat top and bottom for easy stacking, whereas their round sides give them a semirustic appearance.

be approached with caution, though. Wet soil weighs over 100 lb. per cubic foot. For a 4-ft. by 8-ft. bed only 12 in. deep, that works out to more than 1½ tons. Have an architect or engineer assess the structure's ability to carry such a load. If you live in an apartment building, notify the superintendent of your intentions.

If your bed will be placed on a lawn or meadow, you'll need to do some site preparation.

1. Begin by laying out the bed's footprint with string and stakes, powdered lime, or spray paint. Be sure to make the corners square.

2. When the layout is complete, remove strips of turf 2 in. wider than the bed's sides and a couple of inches deep. Outline the strips with a spade, then peel back the turf with a mattock, as shown in **A**, or use a fork or spade to cut out smaller squares. The remaining turf within the confines of the bed will rot when the bed is filled.

3. Where the turf was removed, cut shallow trenches level with the lowest corner (you can eyeball this). If the trench is not level, add gravel where needed to level it out. If there's a substantial grade change from one end of the bed to the other, you may consider using narrower boards in the places where the grade is highest, as shown in **B**. There's no point in burying an entire side board below grade. When the trenches are level and fairly smooth all around, the "foundation" is complete.

Building Staked Beds

Staking the sides of a raised bed transfers outward-thrusting forces to the subsoil below (see the drawing on the facing page). This is a simple

A staked bed depends on the stakes to resist soil pressure. Side boards are mounted on the inside of the stakes so that soil presses the boards against the stakes.

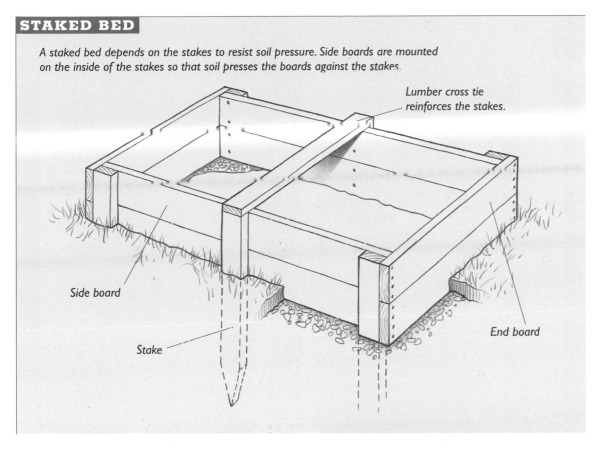

Lumber cross tie reinforces the stakes.

Side board

End board

Stake

and inexpensive way to reinforce a raised bed, but a lot depends on the soil in your area. Marshy soil is too soft to hold stakes securely. At the other extreme, some soil is so rocky that it's practically impossible to drive a stake into it. Stakes work best in firm, homogenous clay, so if you're building over this type of subsoil, a staked bed is a good choice. This bed shouldn't be used on rocky soils, where driving the stakes accurately is a problem, or on rooftops or patios.

1. Line up and drive the stakes to support the sides of the bed. Drive the stakes well below grade for strength. They should penetrate 1½ ft. to 2½ ft. into hard, undisturbed subsoil. The tops of the stakes should all be level. Dig a shallow trench just inside the line of stakes, as shown in **A** (on p. 82). If you plan to cultivate the soil below the bed, leave a 6-in.-wide shelf

A staked bed may look utilitarian, but it's the least expensive raised bed to build. The only difficulty that may arise is driving the stakes.

PRO**TIP**

Point the stakes with a circular saw, clamping them securely to a pair of sawhorses before cutting. It's easier to point both ends of a long piece and then cut it in half, producing two stakes.

TRADE SECRET

If you don't like the look of stakes on the outside of the bed, you can put the side boards outside the stakes, but you will need to fasten them with bolts instead of nails because soil pressure will be constantly pushing the boards away from the stakes. This look is similar to that of a freestanding bed (see the drawing p. 84).

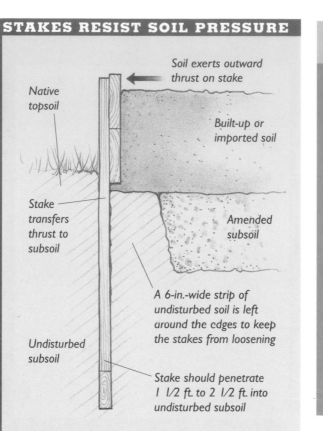

STAKES RESIST SOIL PRESSURE

Native topsoil

Soil exerts outward thrust on stake

Built-up or imported soil

Stake transfers thrust to subsoil

Amended subsoil

Undisturbed subsoil

A 6-in.-wide strip of undisturbed soil is left around the edges to keep the stakes from loosening

Stake should penetrate 1 1/2 ft. to 2 1/2 ft. into undisturbed subsoil

Dealing with Rocky Soil

IN ROCKY SOILS, IT'S DIFFICULT to drive a stake with any kind of accuracy. When the stake hits a rock, it veers off and tilts out of plumb. To some extent, it's possible to pound the stake back on course and continue, but if you're among boulders, a wooden stake will shatter before you reach the necessary depth. For rocky situations, you may be able to use galvanized steel pipe, which can take more of a beating than wooden stakes. Use at least 1-in.-dia. pipes for strength and to provide a significant bearing surface against the soil. Slender lengths of rebar can be driven easily enough, but they are too flexible to perform well as stakes, and their narrow profile is apt to pull through the subsoil rather than bear against it.

A

of undisturbed soil around the edges to avoid weakening your stakes.

PT 2×4 stakes work well in soil that's not too rocky. Cut a long tapering angle on the ends of the stakes for easy penetration. You don't need to dig holes before driving stakes, but if the soil is very hard, stab the ground a few times with a digging bar to give the stake a head start in the right direction.

2. Starting on one of the long sides of the bed, screw the top board to the inside of the stake. Do the same for the other side. Then screw in the lower boards, making sure the fit is snug between the two courses, as shown in **B**.

Wooden stakes should be attached to side boards with galvanized screws or nails, whereas pipe stakes should be attached with galvanized conduit clips. The nails, screws, or conduit clips

used to fasten side boards to the stakes actually become superfluous once the bed is filled and soil pressure takes over.

3. Screw the top courses for the ends to the stakes. Then attach the bottom courses for the ends. Attach a metal strap at the corners for reinforcement, as shown in **C**.

4. Because stakes give the bed most of its support, you probably won't need a cross tie. However, if you're in doubt about the strength of the stakes, you can add a 2×4 cross tie to be on the safe side, as shown in **D**.

Building Freestanding Lumber Beds

When the soil is very rocky or you're building on a rooftop or terrace, you need a freestanding bed. Without stakes to bear the load, however, you must use cross ties to keep the sides from bowing out like a rowboat.

Although 2×4 ties can be used, they are subject to terrific strain at their ends—enough in some cases to tear out the small amount of wood between a fastener and the end of the 2×4. Stronger and less conspicuous ties can be made with long rods that are threaded like bolts (see the drawing on p. 84). Whereas bolts employ a head on one end and a nut on the other end for

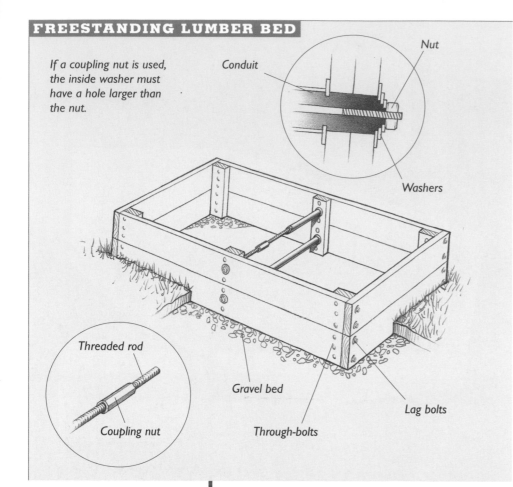

FREESTANDING LUMBER BED

If a coupling nut is used, the inside washer must have a hole larger than the nut.

Nut

Conduit

Washers

Threaded rod

Coupling nut

Gravel bed

Through-bolts

Lag bolts

Log cabin timber beds provide a rustic look in a vegetable garden.

tightening, threaded rods employ two nuts—one on each end. Threaded rods are available in most lumberyards and hardware stores.

Pass the rod through a sleeve of metal electrical conduit to give it some protection from corrosion. The conduit will also lock in the precise width of the bed. Because threaded rods are most commonly sold in 3-ft. lengths, you may need more than one length to span your raised bed. In that case, splice the two rods with a coupling nut. Be sure your metal sleeve is large enough to admit the coupling nut as well as the rod itself. A nominal ¾-in. conduit accommodates a ⅜-in. rod with a coupling nut. The holes you drill should be ⅛ in. to ¼ in. larger in diameter than the rod. If a coupling nut is required you'll need an even bigger hole. Use washers to keep the conduit from being drawn into the hole under tension.

Building Log-Cabin Timber Beds

If you want a rustic look for your garden, a log-cabin bed is the raised bed for you. Landscape timbers lend a natural, Davy Crockett look to the structure, and they have more character than plain boards. They can be constructed of square timbers or semisquare landscape timbers. Their one drawback is that the width of the timbers reduces the available soil space when compared to 2× lumber. On the other hand, having a wide edge on which to park your elbow or derriere while plucking weeds is not a bad idea.

The construction of this type of bed is simplicity itself (see the top drawing on the facing page). There are no cross ties and no special fasteners—just big spikes. The only tools you'll need are a saw, a drill, and a hammer, and the intentionally rough look of this bed means you

FREESTANDING LANDSCAPING TIMBER BED

Timbers are strong enough to resist soil pressure on their own. Cross ties aren't needed unless the bed is more than 8 ft long.

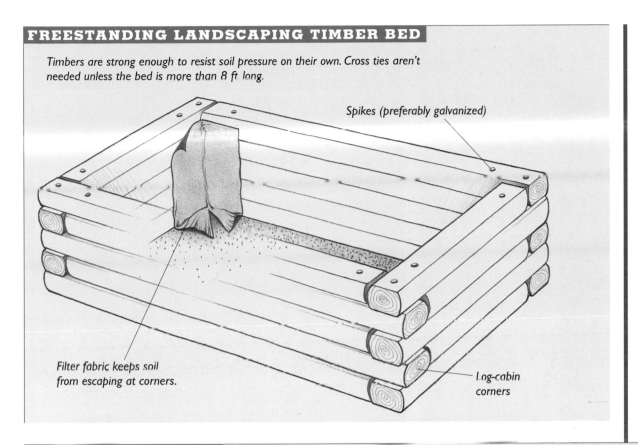

Spikes (preferably galvanized)

Filter fabric keeps soil from escaping at corners.

Log-cabin corners

PLANNING THE CUTS

To simplify cutting, make the length of the timbers the same in all courses.

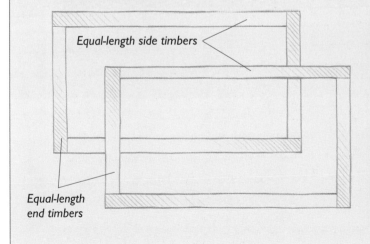

Equal-length side timbers

Equal-length end timbers

It will take longer to cut if you make the length of the timbers alternate from short to long between courses.

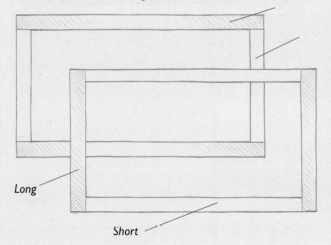

Long

Short

don't have to worry about making perfect cuts. Just be careful when you pick out your landscape timbers; because they are produced from young trees, they are often twisted and warped.

To simplify cutting, make all of the side timbers equal and all of the end timbers equal (see the drawing above).

**The soil used to fill
a raised bed** can be
imported from another
site or can be built up
from scratch by compost-
ing directly in the bed
for several years before
planting.

1. Predrill your timbers before assembly to
make spiking easier.

2. Spike together the first two courses of each
side. Offset the ends by the width of a timber,
as shown in **A**.

3. Overlap the first and second course
subassemblies at one corner and screw them
together, as shown in **B** and the sidebar on the
facing page. Long screws work best for these

four initial corners because the assembly
won't be solid enough at this point to
withstand hammer blows without bouncing
around. After the second course, you will be
able to pound in spikes as fasteners.

4. Spike any subsequent courses in place.
A helper can apply some weight to hold the
timber steady, as shown in **C**.

Log-Cabin Corners

WHEN MAKING LOG-CABIN CORNERS with semisquare landscape timbers, there will be gaps between the square end of each timber and the rounded side of the adjoining timber. To keep soil from leaking out through these gaps, staple filter fabric to the inside of the bed at the corners before filling the bed with soil (see the drawing on p. 85). To avoid gaps altogether, you can miter the corners of landscape-timber beds (see the photo below). Use mend-

Landscape timbers can be log-cabined together (back) or mitered (middle). Concealed metal plates reinforce the miters (front).

Filling the Bed

Before filling a raised bed, consider turning over and amending some of the native soil below the bed. As well as encouraging root growth and the local worm population, this brings certain trace minerals up out of the subsoil. These oft-overlooked nutrients are sometimes absent from topsoil. When spading, don't disturb the soil on which the sides rest.

When a raised bed sits on a hard surface such as a patio, you can improve drainage by putting down a 3-in. layer of small stones or gravel on the bottom of the bed before filling. Then add a layer of filter fabric to isolate gravel from soil. To allow water in the gravel bed to escape, shim up the sides of the bed with a few 20d galvanized spikes laid sideways on the patio. This produces a ¼-in. drainage gap all around the base of the bed.

DESIGN
OPTIONS

▲ The wide flat coping on these raised beds makes a good kneeling surface for the gardener. The coping boards also stiffen the side boards underneath, helping them to resist lateral soil pressure.

◄ A mix of
saplings and
narrow wooden
laths has been
woven together
here to contain
a raised bed—a
delightful use of
material that
might otherwise
be discarded.

▲ These timber
beds have been
neatly con-
structed with log
cabin corners.

◄ Paint can liven
up an otherwise
boring bed. A
coat of purple
paint makes this
wooden patio
bed sizzle.

FENCES

Wooden fence styles run the gamut from crude to refined, with every imaginable variant in between. Choosing a fence for your yard means finding a style that is both functional and visually harmonious with its surroundings.

Beyond taste, there are practical questions to be answered before you can choose the right fence. For most of us, cost will be a controlling factor, but how difficult the fence is to install is also important. Different fences require different levels of skill to build, as well as different tools. Time is another consideration. A fence can be a big project. If time is abundant and money is short, you'll probably want to tackle every phase of the project yourself. But if 9 o'clock tennis sounds better than digging post holes or brushing on stain, you may want to farm out part or all of the work to a contractor or build a simpler fence. ▶ ▶ ▶

Types of Fences

Wood fences can be divided into two broad categories: open fences and screening fences. In more rural areas, open fences are used to delineate broad areas of landscape, but they're also used in suburban settings where privacy is not a concern. Screening fences are typically found in close proximity to homes. They provide privacy between neighbors and block out unsightly views.

Open fences

The two main types of open, or see-through, fences are board fences and post-and-rail fences. The difference lies mainly in their horizontal members. Board fences employ flat boards, whereas post-and-rail fences use chunkier members, such as round poles or square timbers.

Board fences Board fencing is a standard feature of the American landscape (see the photo below). In its simplest form, it consists of posts on 8-ft. centers, with three or four 1×6 rails (horizontal boards) nailed on one side. However, this basic theme can be varied in a number of ways.

Posts for this type of fence are usually rough-sawn 4×4s. Round posts can be used, but they won't provide good bearing for the boards (see the left drawings on the facing page). To compensate for this, you can cut shallow notches into the posts or try half-round posts. The flat side of a half-round post provides a good nailing surface, whereas the round side has a more natural look to it than a square post. Half-round posts also cost less than square. Nailing a vertical 1×6 cover board on top of a half-round post dresses up the fence and gives the post more visual weight.

Board fencing graces the pasture along this rural roadside.

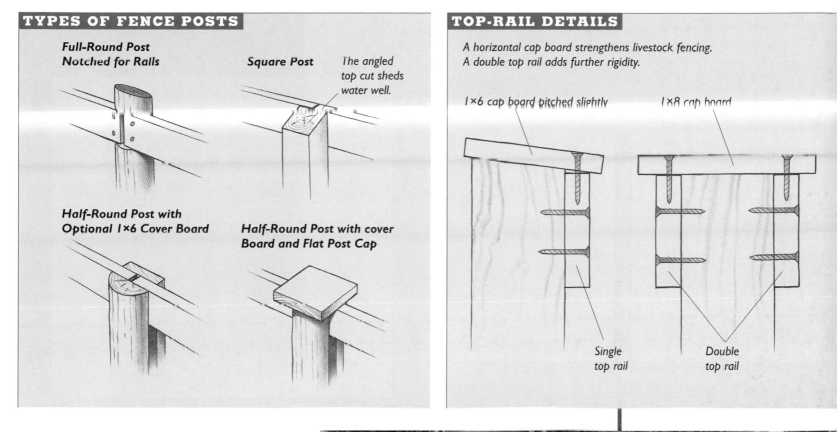

TYPES OF FENCE POSTS

Full-Round Post Notched for Rails

Square Post

The angled top cut sheds water well.

Half-Round Post with Optional 1×6 Cover Board

Half-Round Post with cover Board and Flat Post Cap

TOP-RAIL DETAILS

A horizontal cap board strengthens livestock fencing. A double top rail adds further rigidity.

1×6 cap board pitched slightly

1×8 cap board

Single top rail

Double top rail

Rails are produced in pressure-treated yellow pine and unseasoned oak. The PT product has greater decay resistance, but the oak has much greater strength. Rails are typically roughsawn, measuring a full 1 in. by 6 in. by 16 ft. long. To strengthen the fence, stagger the joints between rails so they don't all fall on a single post. To strengthen the top rail, nail a flat cover board to its edge to create a member with an L cross section (see the right drawings above). Combining the cover board with an additional rail on the other side of the post will make an even stronger U-shaped assembly.

Although rails usually run horizontally, a handsome board fence can be achieved with a cross-buck pattern (see the photo at right). Or the spacing between horizontal boards can be varied to produce different effects.

Post-and-rail fences The post-and-rail fence is a cousin of the board fence. In this type of

A board fence with cross-buck rails strays from the ordinary.

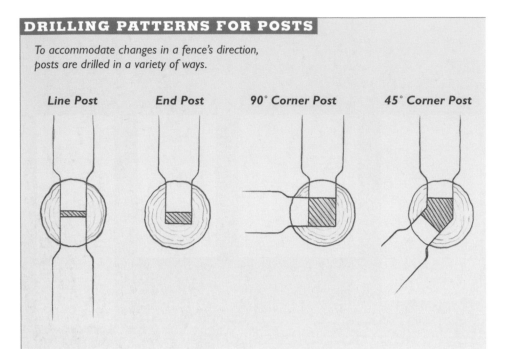

Line Post   End Post   90° Corner Post   45° Corner Post

A square-cornered post-and-rail fence creates a geometric look.

TRADE SECRET

If you feel comfortable with rough carpentry but not finish work, build a simple fence or buy a fancy prefabricated panel that you can apply to your own rough substructure.

fence, the rail fits into a recess in the post instead of being nailed on. Posts are usually round, with circular or oblong holes to receive the rails. To allow a fence to change directions, posts are drilled in a variety of ways (see the drawings above). Prepare a list of the different types of posts you need before you talk to your fence supplier.

The rails are either full round or quarter round and may have either a dowel end for round holes or a scarfed end for oblong holes. Square-cornered post-and-rail systems are also available for a more geometric look (see the photo above).

Screening fences

Screening fences can be used for privacy or to obscure unsavory items such as trash cans. Most screening fences consist of three elements: vertical posts, horizontal rails, and vertical pickets, or pales.

There are many versions of this type of fence. Posts can be partially or completely covered

over on one side by the pickets, or they may be exposed on both sides if rails run between the posts. It's the pickets, though, that establish a fence's identity through their color, texture, size, shape, and spacing. You can buy prefabricated fence panels or build your own fence on site from scratch.

Picket fences A picket fence, which is typically 2 ft. to 3 ft. tall, is often employed around a yard or garden. Posts are typically 4×4, 6 ft. to 8 ft. on center, and the rails are 2×4. The pickets are usually 1×3 or 1×4, with the tops cut in a decorative pattern. Narrow 1×1 pickets can also be used—closely spaced, they impart an aristocratic air (see the top photo on the facing page). You can buy prefabricated panels for a picket

A rustic picket
fence of rough-
sawn oak creates
a unique, natural
look. Square-
topped pickets
alternate with
spear points.

fence, but I've found that the panels often leave
too much space between the pickets, so consider
building your own.

One of the chief delights of the picket fence
is the variety of ways in which the pickets can
be arranged. Although a straight horizontal line
across the top is common, there are many alter-
natives that can enliven the end product without substantially increasing its cost. For country
gardens, rustic picket fences made of sticks and
branches look great. Because of the irregularity of the sticks, nailing can be difficult, but you
can use galvanized wire lashing wrapped tightly
around your sticks instead of nails. The use of
roughsawn lumber can also lend a rustic air to a
picket fence (see the photo right).

Vertical-board fences A vertical-board fence
provides maximum privacy. It is usually 6 ft. tall,
with three 2×4 or 2×6 rails between posts. The
posts are set 7 ft. or 8 ft. on center. You can buy
prefabricated panels or assemble this type of
fence piece by piece.

If you're using prefabricated panels and you
want the panels' rails to be the sole support for
the pickets, you must place the posts very carefully so that the panels join directly over the
centerline of each post (see the drawings on
p. 96); otherwise, you may have a partial picket

Prefabricated vertical-board fence panels can be mounted directly on posts, but the spacing of the posts must then be close to perfect. To accommodate irregular post spacing, attach subrails to the posts first. The panels can then hang on the subrails, independent of the posts.

Panels Over Posts (No Subrails)

Joints between panels must occur at posts.

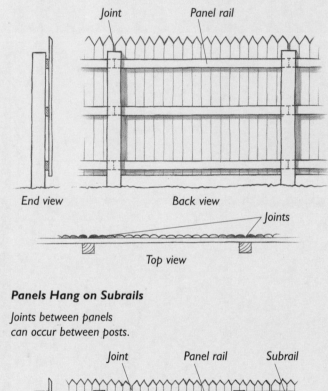

Panels Hang on Subrails

Joints between panels can occur between posts.

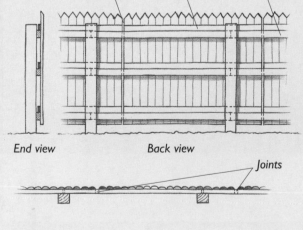

or a gap where the panels join. To permit greater flexibility in the spacing of the posts, build a substructure of posts and subrails and then hang the panels consecutively on this substructure, regardless of the post placement. In this system, the rail that comes with the panel serves merely to hold the pickets together. To attach the panel to the substructure, nail through every fifth or sixth picket.

If you opt to build the panels yourself, the pickets—which are usually 1×6—can be applied in a variety of ways (see the drawings on the facing page). The tops can be trimmed in any style you like (for more on making pickets, see the sidebar on p. 106). For a finished appearance on both sides of the fence, apply pickets to both sides. Two sets of pickets double the weight on the rails, so either increase the size of the rails or build diagonal braces into the substructure. The braces have a truss effect that keeps the rails from sagging. To create a same-on-both-sides fence without the extra weight and expense of double pickets, you can stagger a single set of pickets (see the photo on the facing page).

Stockade fences A stockade fence draws its inspiration from the palisade forts built on the American frontier. It is sold in panel form only. The pickets for this type of fence are tightly spaced half-round poles, about 3 in. in diameter, with pointed tops. Balsam fir is a popular species, as are spruce and cedar. The bark, which peels off eventually, is sometimes left on for an especially rustic look.

Louver fences A louver fence is made for privacy, with horizontal slats arranged on a downward slant, and has a breezy, contemporary look. You can mill grooves in the posts to receive the slats; simply toenail the slats in place, or use a metal clip to hold the slats (see the drawings on p. 98).

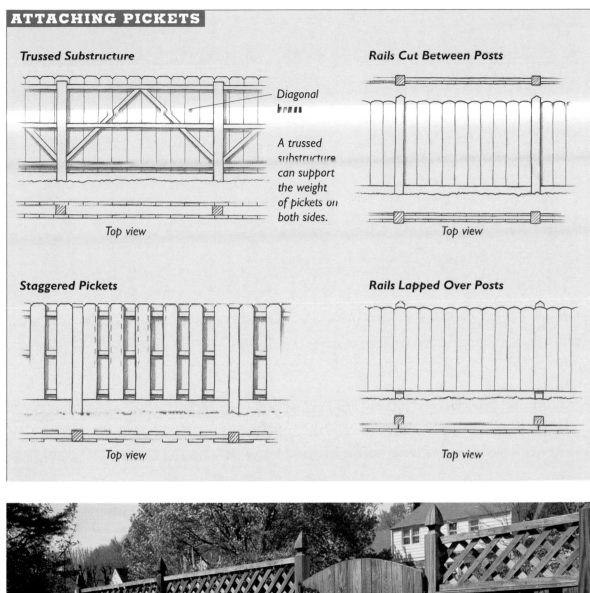

ATTACHING PICKETS

Trussed Substructure

Diagonal brace

Top view

A trussed substructure can support the weight of pickets on both sides.

Rails Cut Between Posts

Top view

Staggered Pickets

Top view

Rails Lapped Over Posts

Top view

This privacy fence has staggered pickets on both sides. A lattice "topper" extends the height of the fence without being overbearing.

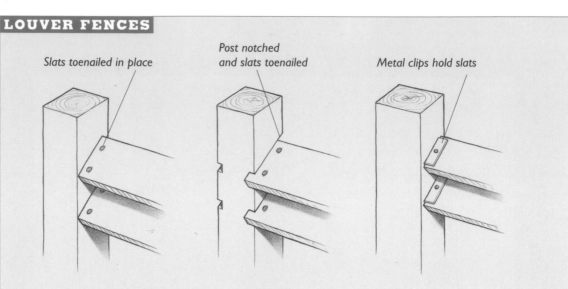

Slats toenailed in place

Post notched
and slats toenailed

Metal clips hold slats

Slats for a louvered fence can be toenailed to the posts (left), inserted in notches in the posts and toenailed (middle), or attached to the posts with metal clips (right).

TRADE SECRET

Trimming the top of a solid panel with a band of lattice (called a topper) produces a graceful look with full screening where it's needed most.

This lattice-panel fence conceals a propane tank.

The posts for this type of fence shouldn't be too far apart, or the slats will sag. If you choose 1×4 or 1×6 slats, the maximum spacing would be about 6 ft. For 2×4 or 2×6 slats, you can increase the spacing to 10 ft.

Panel fences A panel fence is typically prefabricated and is available in many forms. For complete privacy, you can get panels consisting of solid boards laid tightly together within a frame. Another type has thin bands of wood woven closely together like a basket. The most common prefabricated panel is lattice, which offers partial screening without the heavy look of a solid fence (see the photo at left).

Lattice panels are available in ½-in. and 1-in. thicknesses, which refers to the combined thick-

ness of the overlapping battens. For example, ½-in. lattice has ¼-in.-thick battens, and 1-in. lattice has ½-in.-thick battens. The heavy material works best because it's strong and because the staples holding the lattice strips together have more to bite into. Premium lattice stock also has rounded corners.

Wood lattice is available in PT yellow pine and cedar. For low maintenance, vinyl lattice is also available. You can apply lattice diagonally, for a diamond pattern, or horizontally, in a tic-tac-toe motif.

To hold lattice panels in place, use 2×2 channel stock, which has a wide groove that engages the edge of the lattice. The channel stock can be fastened to rails and posts. The same effect can be achieved by nailing 1×1 stops on both sides of the panel.

Lattice panels are sold in 4×8 sheets. To create a 6-ft.-high fence, you can span the open space below the panel with closely spaced 1×4s or plant shrubbery.

Fence Construction

Once you've chosen the style of your fence, it's time to get down to work. First you'll need to lay out the fence line. The sweatiest part of the job will be digging holes for all the posts (for more information on digging post holes, see Chapter 2) and then setting and trimming them. Now the carpentry begins. You'll need to install horizontal boards or rails at the very least. When building a screening fence, you'll also be attaching vertical pickets to the rails or hanging prefabricated panels between the posts.

The instructions that follow are for a basic picket fence, but you can dress it up in a number of ways. Try changing the shape of the pickets, their height, or their spacing. Adding post finials can spice up the design as well.

Whatever your particular style, you can use this basic plan to build your own picket fence. It's really easy. If you keep the pickets close together and space them evenly, your fence will turn out fine. You can simplify the construction by nailing the rails to the outside of the posts rather than running them between posts, but the appearance won't be quite as neat.

Laying out the fence line

Before you do any digging you must determine the layout of your fence.

1. Locate the ends of the fence as well as any corners or changes in the fence's direction. Drive a stake at each location, then tie string between the stakes.

2. Once the fence line is established, mark the location of intermediate posts. Maximum spacing will depend on the strength of the rails you're using. Adjust the spacing of the posts so that you don't have a short oddball section left over at the end of a run. The exception is a fence made of prefabricated panels, which may be difficult to adjust in width. When building a panel fence, it may be best to coordinate the post spacing carefully with the panels, even if that means relocating the ends or corners of the fence.

Installing posts

Once you've marked the post locations, dig the post holes and begin setting the posts.

1. Start with the corner posts. Dig the post holes with a post-hole digger. In tough soil, use a digging bar to loosen dirt, shear through roots, and dislodge stones, as shown in **A**.

2. Set the posts in the post holes, plumb them with a spirit level, and brace them in two directions to hold them during backfilling. (The tops of the posts will be trimmed later, so don't worry about a difference in height at this point.) Tack the braces near the top of the fence post at one end and nail them to a tree or to a stake in the ground at the other end. Now pull a string between the corner posts to guide the position of the intermediate posts, as shown in **B** and the drawing at left.

3. Measure off the locations of the intermediate posts with a tape measure and mark them with lime. After digging the holes, set each post with its face parallel to the string. Nudge them close to the stringline, using a 2×4 as a lever, as

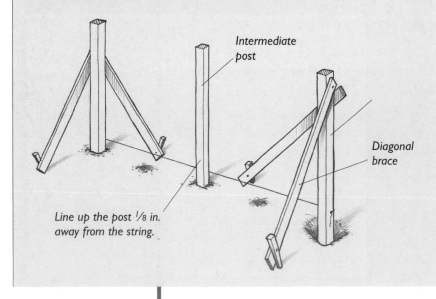

SETTING POSTS

Diagonal braces hold the corner posts plumb. Stretch string between the corners to guide the setting of the intermediate posts.

Intermediate post

Diagonal brace

Line up the post ⅛ in. away from the string.

shown in . Leave a ¼-in. gap between the stringline and all the posts to avoid accumulated error.

4. Pack concrete around the posts and agitate it with a stick to eliminate voids. A fairly stiff mix will support the post best, as shown in **D**. Plumb each post as its hole is backfilled.

Trimming posts

Once the concrete has hardened, trim the posts to a uniform height, which will make the fence run parallel to grade. Trimming the posts after they're installed is easier than trying to set all of them at exactly the same height in the first place.

Measure the height of each post above grade. Using the shortest post as the standard, cut off all the posts at the same height with a small chainsaw or a handsaw (see the bottom photo at right). Cut the tops at a slight angle (about 10 degrees) so that they'll shed water quicker (see the left drawing on p. 93). An even more effective way to protect the top of a post is to nail on a short piece of board as a sloping lid or attach a beveled

post cap (for more on making post caps, see the sidebar on p. 102).

Although making the fence run parallel to grade is generally desirable, the location of a post may fall in a sudden dip in the landscape. Rather than transfer this sudden aberration in grade to the fence line, determine where to cut by pulling a string between neighboring posts. The intervening post can then be cut off according to the line, rather than according to grade. Consequently, these special posts will be taller

Trim the tops of the posts after the concrete has hardened. Stretch a stringline between the corner posts to mark the cuts.

Shaping Post Caps

A post cap can be beveled with a block plane.

POST CAPS CAN BE AS SIMPLE AS a block of 2×6 nailed to a 4×4 post, but with a little extra effort you can produce shaped post caps that look better and last longer.

Post caps can be profiled in different ways. You can work a simple bevel on the cap with a block plane (see the photo above). You can also cut corner bevels on a table-saw with the blade tilted to 45 degrees. If you have a router, you can mold the edges of the post cap. To hold the cap securely while you rout the edges, use brads to temporarily tack the cap to a heavy plank. Make sure the brads are placed far enough from the edge to avoid hitting them with the router bit.

A popular post-cap shape is a low pyramid, often with a finial at the top. The practical advantage of this design is that it sheds water faster than a flat post cap does. To produce the pyramid shape, tilt the blade of your tablesaw about 5 degrees. You will be running the square post cap past the blade on edge (see the top photo at right). To steady the work, fasten a high auxiliary fence to your table-saw's regular fence. (The regular fence should have holes, allowing you to screw through the regular fence into the auxiliary fence.) Guide the post cap past the blade, pushing with one hand while using a push stick in the other to press the work against the fence.

The tops of the posts can also be pointed by cutting a bevel on all four sides (see the bottom photo at right). Pointed posts are difficult to trim in place, so the beveling should be done before installation. In that case, you'll need to set the posts at the correct height initially.

You can saw a pyramid-shaped post cap on a tablesaw. Just be sure to use a push stick to keep your hand away from the blade.

To point the end of a post, make a bevel cut on each side.

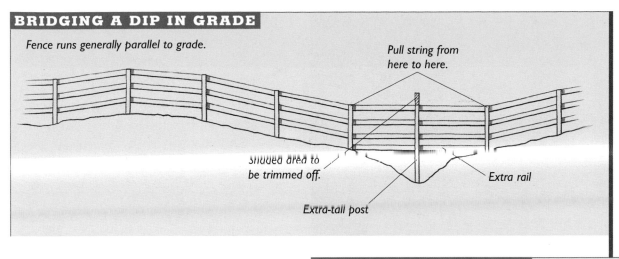

BRIDGING A DIP IN GRADE

Fence runs generally parallel to grade.

Pull string from here to here.

Shaded area to be trimmed off.

Extra rail

Extra-tall post

than the others in order to maintain a graceful line (see the drawing above).

Prefabricated panel fences cannot, by their nature, run parallel to grade. Instead, they must be installed in a stepped arrangement. To trim posts for such a fence, measure the drop in grade between neighboring post locations with a spirit level and straightedge. The process is similar to gauging variations in post-hole depth (see the drawing on p. 133). Add the drop-in-grade distance to the standard post height, plus a little extra for trimming, to find the length of each post.

Marking rails

After trimming the posts, you need to figure out the location of the rails.

1. Make a measuring stick from a smooth, slender board. Let one end of the stick represent finish grade. Cut off the other end so that the stick's length equals the height of a standard post above grade. Then mark lines to represent the positions of the rails. An X indicates which side of the mark the rail will go on.

2. Stand the stick up next to each post and transfer your marks to the post (see the draw-

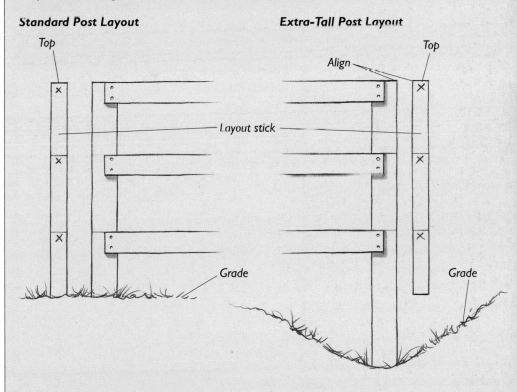

USING A LAYOUT STICK

Use a layout stick to establish the height of the posts and the spacing of the rails. Where sudden dips or rises occur, use a string (see the drawing above) as the reference point on the post instead of grade.

Standard Post Layout

Top

Layout stick

Grade

Extra-Tall Post Layout

Align

Top

Layout stick

Grade

ings above). If any extra-tall posts have been installed, as mentioned previously, you should use the tops of the neighboring posts as a reference when laying out the rails, rather than using grade as a reference.

Line up the bottom rails with the marks on the posts, then toenail the bottom rails to the posts.

Attaching rails

Fence rails may be fitted between posts and toenailed or simply face-nailed to one side of the post. Fitting rails between posts is more difficult, because the rails must be cut to fit tightly and because toenailing is tricky (see the photo at left). For these reasons, installing the rail between posts is generally reserved for more formal styles, such as picket fences. There are three basic methods of installing rails between posts (see the drawings below).

Making the pickets

If you're cutting out individual pickets, use a handsaw or a portable power saw. Make a pattern from picket stock or something lighter, such as ¼-in. plywood. Trace the pattern onto each piece to guide the cut. Or, to avoid having to measure each piece, set up a stop block, which is a block of wood nailed or clamped to the workbench a

PROTIP

Radial-arm saws and chopsaws are effective for mass-producing simple, pointed pickets.

FLUSH RAIL-TO-POST CONNECTIONS

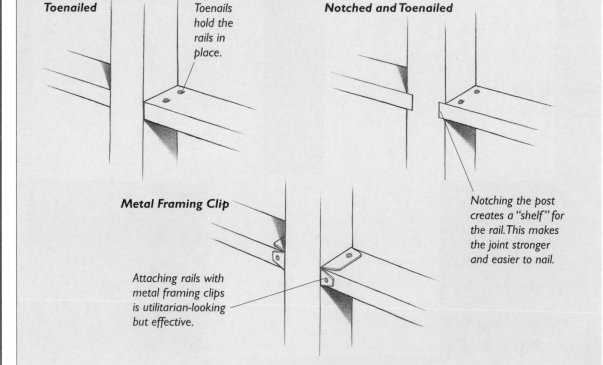

Toenailed

Toenails hold the rails in place.

Notched and Toenailed

Notching the post creates a "shelf" for the rail. This makes the joint stronger and easier to nail.

Metal Framing Clip

Attaching rails with metal framing clips is utilitarian-looking but effective.

Nailing It Right

Make the picket points with a chop-saw. Fasten a stop block to the bench (seen at far right in the photo) to regulate the length of the picket and to avoid repeated measurements.

set distance from the sawblade. By snugging the end of the picket stock against this block, you can cut each picket the same length. Also, by angling the sawblade you can cut the pointy end of the picket without doing any layout. A single angle cut makes a sawtooth picket, whereas flipping the piece for a second cut produces a spear-tipped picket. To make a square 1×1 picket with a pyramid tip, rotate the piece four times.

Attaching pickets

If you're building a picket fence, install the pickets after the rails are on.

1. Nail on the first picket, then check it with a level to make sure it's plumb. For standard ¾-in.-thick pickets, use 6d common nails, two at the top and two at the bottom. To maintain a constant distance between the top of the picket and the edge of the top rail, either measure with a ruler or make a gauge block. The block simply sits on top of the rail to guide you in setting the picket. You can make a separate gauge block to regulate the spacing between pickets or combine the two gauges (see the

A

The top of a picket is aligned with a gauge block that sits on the rail behind it.

bottom photo above and the drawing on p. 107).).

2. Continue installing pickets along the fence line. Every so often, use a level to check the last picket installed for plumb. If it's out of plumb, compensate slightly over the next several pickets until you're back on track. The eye won't readily detect minor deviations from plumb,

Fence Picket Shapes

Pickets can be cut with a jigsaw after they're installed.

Use a thin batten to trace a curved line on the row of pickets. Then trim the pickets in place with a jigsaw.

YOU CAN BUY OFF-THE-SHELF FENCE PICKETS in a few basic patterns, but you can make much more interesting ones yourself. To find a pattern you like, search the architecture section of your library. If you live near a town with fine old homes, take a walking tour. Better yet, design something yourself.

You can either precut your fancy pickets or install oversize pickets and then trim their tops in place. A jigsaw works well for this, but you should try this technique only if you feel comfortable using a jigsaw in a vertical position. If the tops of the pickets are to line up in a straight line, install the oversize pickets and then snap a horizontal chalkline at the desired height. Trace the pattern onto each picket in accordance with the chalkline, and cut them out (see the top photo above).

You can also trim the pickets along a curve, again using a jigsaw. Set nails at the high points of the curve, letting them stick out about 1 in. Then flex a thin wood batten into position between the nails and trace a line along the batten (see the bottom photo above). Cut directly along this curve or hold a pattern to each picket so that the points of the pickets align along the curve.

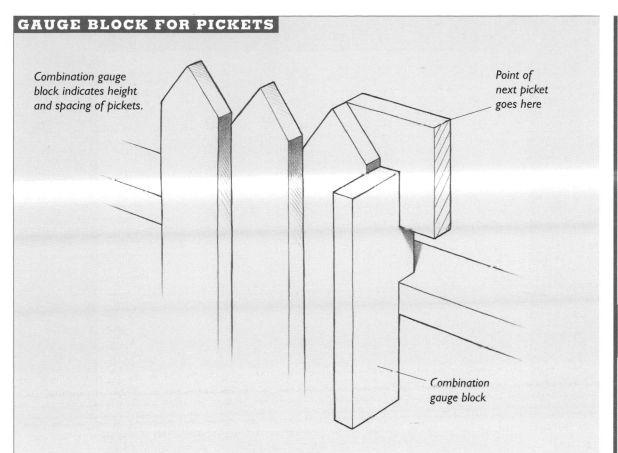

Combination gauge block indicates height and spacing of pickets.

Point of next picket goes here

Combination gauge block

but a sudden change of spacing to make a correction will stand out. Keep the bottoms of the pickets at least 4 in. above grade to keep them out of the dew and to permit a string trimmer to pass underneath when cutting grass.

It's best to terminate each run of fence with a full picket, so keep this in mind as you approach the end of a run. To determine if you need to modify your spacing to ensure a full picket, cut a layout stick about 6 ft. long, hold the stick next to the pickets you have already installed, and mark off their positions. Holding this stick against the unfinished portion of the fence will tell you where the pickets will fall at your current spacing. You can then figure out whether you should tighten the spacing or open it up a little.

Finishing a fence

In naturalized settings, no finish will be required. All woods eventually turn a silvery gray, which fits well with most landscapes. On the other hand, fences close to a home may require paint or stain to harmonize with existing structures. You can apply the finish with a brush, roller, or spray (for more on finishes, see pp. 23-25).

TRADE SECRET

Don't paint the posts where they show between the pickets, or at least paint them a dark color. You want it to look like there's a space between the pickets, and painting the post the same color as the fence will cause the pickets to run together visually.

DESIGN
OPTIONS

▲ Macho masonry meets wispy wood, creating a great contrast—and balance.

▶ The pickets on this cedar fence have been spaced slightly apart, making it less foreboding than a solid fence. The lattice topper with a doubled top rail adds elegance.

◀ The elegant formality of a house in town extends to this fence along the street.

◀ The inventive builder of this fence has used peeled cedar saplings to render a different design on each panel.

◀ This whimsical garden fence features birdhouse posts and narrow, pyramid-top pickets. Curved fence rails such as these can be sawn with a jigsaw.

GATES

A gate can make a strong opening statement about a home and its occupants. Whatever the fence says, the gate should say it with an exclamation point. In addition to style, transparency is an issue on which the fence and the gate should agree. A see-through picket fence calls for a similarly friendly entrance, whereas a solid panel fence or a stone wall wants the guarded opacity of a solid gate or an open gate with thick, heavy members.

A gate is more than just the aesthetic focal point of a fence. It's also the fence's hardest working part. Meanwhile, only one side of the gate is supported, whereas the other side hangs in midair. You might say a gate has to do twice the work of an ordinary fence panel with only half the support. Gaining an understanding of the stresses at work on gates and gateposts will help you build a solid gate that will stand the test of time. ▶ ▶ ▶

Types of Gates

The simplest type of gate has flat horizontal rails and diagonal braces fastened to vertical pickets. Any flat board used to tie other boards together in this fashion is called a cleat, so this type of gate is known as "cleated" (see the drawing below). The cleats should be fastened with plenty of screws, but you can substitute clinched nails for

screws if you want a rough-looking gate. Plain nailing will be ineffective here because the flat pickets won't provide enough meat for the nails to sink into.

The other common way to build a gate is by constructing a frame and then covering the frame with pickets. This is called a framed, or box, gate (see the right drawing below). Frame members are usually butted together, with the stiles (vertical members) fitted in between the top and bottom rails. Because a frame has ample thickness, you can use nails to fasten the pickets to the frame instead of screws. But you should use long, coarse-thread screws to secure the corner joints for maximum strength. Also, attach galvanized steel L-plates to the corners, because even screws have limited strength when driven into end grain. Braces should fit snug within the frame and be fastened with long screws as well. A framed gate requires more labor and material than a cleated gate, but the finished product feels heftier and has a more substantial look.

This cottage gate welcomes the humblest pilgrim, muddy boots and all.

GATE TYPES

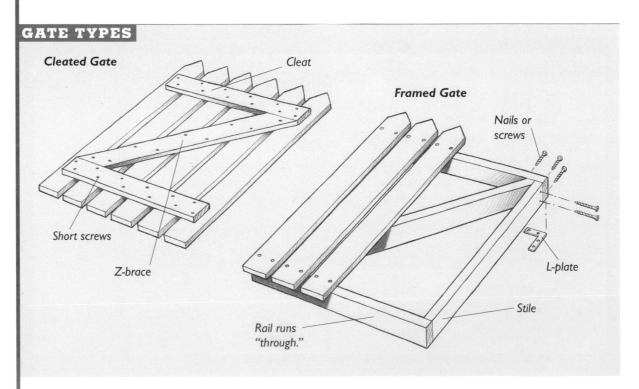

Cleated Gate

Cleat

Short screws

Z-brace

Framed Gate

Nails or screws

L-plate

Stile

Rail runs "through."

Planning Considerations

To meet the aesthetic and functional requirements of a good gate, it's wise to invest in some careful planning. An accurate scale drawing is essential for working out the details of your gate design. If the gate has a unique infill pattern, make a full-scale rendering on a sheet of plywood, then transfer the cutting angles for the various members directly from the sheet to the pieces being cut.

It's a good idea to buy your gate hardware and have it in front of you as you work out the design. The reasons for this are both aesthetic and practical. For instance, wide strap hinges can make a strong visual statement, but they should be sized carefully in proportion to the gate. Meanwhile, different types of latches and hinges mount in different ways. The choice of hardware can also have an effect on the clearance between the gate and gatepost. You don't want any surprises after you've constructed the gate.

Braces

An overriding concern in gate design is diagonal bracing. Because gates are supported on the hinge side only, the unsupported latch side tends to sag. The wider a gate is in relation to its height, the greater the strain will be, because the weight of the latch side is amplified through leverage. You can combat the problem of sagging in a variety of ways, depending on the gate style. Cleated gates may not need a brace, as long as you use wide rails (8 in. or wider) and plenty of fasteners to maximize their grip on a comparatively small area.

Z-Brace The most common solution for sagging is a Z-brace (see the drawings at right). If the Z-brace runs from the top of the latch side to the bottom of the hinge side, the brace is in compression. If the brace runs from the bottom

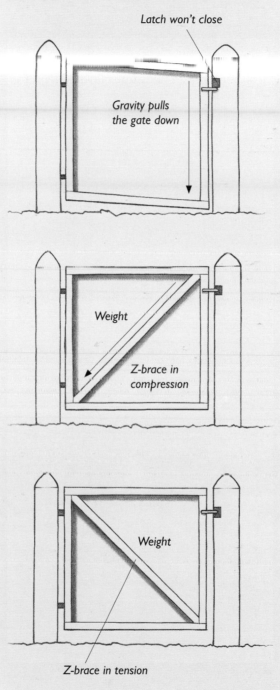

BRACING A GATE

Gravity causes an unbraced gate to sag (top drawing). Adding some sort of diagonal bracing will stiffen the gate, keeping its corners square (middle and bottom drawings).

Latch won't close

Gravity pulls the gate down

Weight

Z-brace in compression

Weight

Z-brace in tension

PRO TIP

The key to building a strong gate—framed or cleated—is to be sure the braces are well fastened to prevent sagging. Screws are the best fasteners for that job.

of the latch side to the top of the hinge side, the brace is in tension. There is a prevailing opinion that wooden gate braces work better in compression than in tension, because that arrangement throws more weight against the bottom of the gatepost, where the post is strongest. However, either arrangement works, as long as all the members are joined securely together.

A Z-brace that runs from corner to corner gives maximum support and should always be used for wide gates. Narrower gates can be adequately stiffened with shorter braces running between adjacent sides, opening up the middle of the gate for other design possibilities. Just be sure that when you add a brace it's diagonal; vertical and horizontal members won't stiffen the gate.

Braces don't have to be straight. A gently curved brace will do most of the work of a straight brace, as long as it's not too narrow (see the photo below). A narrow curving brace, however, is apt to split because its contoured edges cut across the grain of the wood.

The braces on this gate turn out with a subtle flare. The result is a country gate with panache.

Wire Brace If the look of a solid brace is objectionable, use a slender wire brace in conjunction with a turnbuckle. If the gate sags, you can simply tighten the turnbuckle to bring the gate back into squareness. Because wire has plenty of tensile strength but no compressive strength, wire braces must run from the top of the hinge side to the bottom of the latch side. You can use aircraft cable to make a wire brace or a slender rod-and-turnbuckle brace made specifically for screen doors. The rod-and-turnbuckle type has the neater appearance, but it may be too long for your gate. To shorten the rod, cut it with a hacksaw. Once the length is right, hammer the end of the rod on a hard surface to flatten it and drill screw holes through the flattened end.

Infill For a solid gate, consider running infill boards diagonally for stiffness to avoid the need for bracing. You can also glue a wide plywood panel into a gate to prevent sagging. Plywood doesn't hold up well in exposed locations, but for gates with some sort of roof or covering arch, plywood is a good choice. Be sure to use pressure-treated or marine-grade plywood to protect the gate from wind-driven rain. Groove the unsightly edges of the panel into the stiles and rails or conceal them behind stop moldings.

If you want the benefits of both an open and a solid gate, consider a half-and-half design, with solid infill below and spaced pickets or lattice above. The upper section affords transparency where it's most important—looking toward the horizon—whereas the lower panel provides stiffness. For strength, the lower section is sometimes reinforced with a cross buck—a pair of crossed framing members running between opposing corners (see the top photo on the facing page).

Joinery If your gate design won't abide any type of bracing, you'll be depending entirely on the rigidity of the gate's corner joints. One join-

A cross buck in the lower half of each gate provides good bracing. Pickets in the upper half permit a glimpse of the home beyond.

ery method, known as mortise and tenon, is so strong that it can support gates with little or no bracing (depending on the width of the gate). Unfortunately, mortise-and-tenon joints are beyond the skills and equipment of most ama teurs. If you want this type of gate but lack the skills to build it, consult a cabinetmaker about building it for you.

Gateposts

Gateposts have a constant strain imposed upon them by the weight of the gate. When the gate is closed, this weight is transferred to the adjoining fence. When the gate is swung open, however, the weight of the gate wants to pull the post sideways. To counteract this tendency, a gate-post needs to be planted deeper—and be more solidly backfilled—than a regular fence post. In the case of a very wide or heavy gate, the gate-post may need to be increased in thickness as well. Otherwise, the gatepost is liable to bend at ground level, causing the gate to sag and, eventu-ally, to drag on the ground.

Dig holes for gateposts at least 3 ft. deep. For gates wider than 3 ft., dig the holes as deep as the gate is wide, or as deep as you can reach

This gate provides a bold focal point for a rural landscape.

with the equipment at your disposal (for more on digging post holes, see p. 35). Hang gates up to 3 ft. wide on 4-in.-thick posts, gates up to 5 ft. wide on 6-in.-thick posts, and wider gates on 8-in.-thick posts. Increasing the height of a gatepost can give better leverage to the brace, but it places even greater strain on the post, so be sure to use a stout post (see the photo on p. 116).

The diameter of a gatepost hole should be larger than for a fence post for better anchorage, and the hole should be backfilled with concrete.

The height of this gatepost affords good leverage to the brace. The stoutness of the post enables it to withstand the extra strain exerted on the post by this arrangement.

PRO**TIP**

When assembling box posts use a water-resistant glue such as Titebond III®. To keep the corners of the post aligned during assembly it helps to use biscuits–special manufactured wooden wafers that bridge the joint between two boards. A special power tool called a biscuit joiner is used to cut slots for the biscuits.

HOLLOW BOX POST

A hollow box post provides a smooth, formal appearance. The box post slips over a PT solid post that's been planted in concrete.

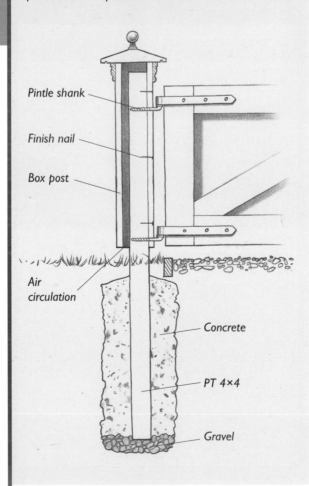

Pintle shank

Finish nail

Box post

Air circulation

Concrete

PT 4×4

Gravel

If the hole isn't large enough, the hardened concrete plug surrounding the gatepost is apt to cut through the soil when the gatepost is strained. Make the gatepost hole at least four times the thickness of the post.

To make a gate more stylish, you can hang it on a painted hollow box post. A box post made from seasoned boards won't develop surface checks like a solid unseasoned post will. The corners of a box post should be glued and nailed well with finish nails. Screws are even stronger, but they will need to be plugged for appearance's sake (for more on plugging screw holes, see the sidebar on the facing page).

Properly constructed box posts have almost as much strength as solid posts of the same size. However, it isn't wise to set a box post below grade because moisture from the ground will get inside and cause it to decay more quickly. The solution is to bury a PT solid post and then slip the hollow box post over it (see the drawing at left). Make the inside dimensions of the box post greater than the outside dimensions of the solid post for a comfortable fit. When installing the gate, make sure the hinges are fastened through the box post into the solid post for support.

Plugging Screw Holes

YOU CAN BUY WOODEN PLUGS FROM mail-order woodworking catalogs and good hardware stores. You can also buy a tool called a plug cutter for making your own wood plugs. A plug cutter is a sort of hollow drill bit that fits in a drill press and is driven into a board to produce a plug of a given size. One of the nice things about making your own plugs is that you can use a decay-resistant wood for exterior work.

1. To plug a screw hole, begin by drilling a counterbore (a hole about ⅛ in. larger than the screw head) in the piece being fastened. The depth of the counterbore should be about one-third the thickness of the board.

2. After drilling the counterbore, finish drilling through the board with a bit whose diameter is smaller than the head of the screw but larger than the screw's shank. Sink the screw.

3. After the screw is installed, glue a wooden plug into the counterbore, leaving the top of the plug slightly above the surface (a condition known as "proud").

4. When the glue has dried, plane off the excess wood to within a shaving's thickness and then sand the plug flush.

Leave the plug proud, then plane and sand it flush.

½-in. counterbore

³/16-in. clearance hole

To hide a wood screw, sink it below the surface, then fill the hole with a wooden plug.

Leave an airspace between the bottom of the box post and the ground to keep water from wicking into the box post's end grain and to allow some air to circulate inside.

Hardware

The choice of gate hardware at most hardware stores leans toward functional-but-ugly types made of stamped galvanized steel. If you are going to the trouble of building a custom gate, you might consider purchasing wrought-iron hardware instead. It's harder to find and a lot more expensive than stamped hardware but much better looking. If there are any blacksmiths in your area, they may be able to forge custom hardware to your specifications.

A hand-forged iron gate latch harmonizes with this weathered oak gate.

PRO TIP

The boards used for hollow posts should be primed on both sides before assembly to keep them from warping. Just don't prime the areas where glue will be applied.

WHAT CAN GO WRONG

Hollow posts and columns can rot unless ventilation is provided to dry up internal moisture. The moisture comes not only from penetrating rain, but also from condensation caused by temperature changes. To maximize ventilation there should be air holes at both the top and the bottom of the post or column.

Butt Hinge

Butt hinges can be face mounted or edge mounted. For a tight fit, the leaves of the hinge can be recessed flush with the wood's surface.

T-Hinge

T-hinges are easy to apply. The rectangular leaf is usually mounted on the gatepost and the tapered leaf is mounted on the gate.

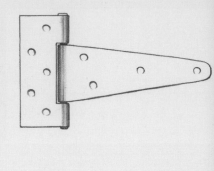

Pintle Hinge

Pintle hinges can be mounted on round gateposts as well as square ones. The type shown has a lag-threaded shank, but machine-threaded versions are also available. Straps can be fancy, such as this heart-tipped pattern, or plain.

COMPENSATING FOR HINGE PLAY

To prevent a sagging gate, wedge the gate in a cockeyed position while you set the hinges. (The position is exaggerated here for clarity.)

When wedges are removed, the gate hangs level

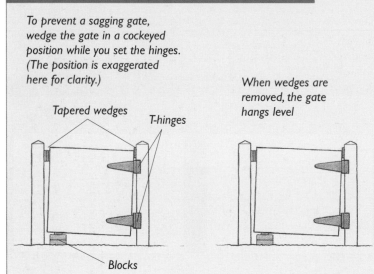

Tapered wedges

T-hinges

Blocks

Hinges No matter what type of gate you choose to build, it needs to swing on a set of hinges. So let's take a look at the three most common gate hinges (see the top drawings above): butt hinges, T-hinges, and pintle hinges.

Butt hinges are the square hinges typically used to hang house doors. You can easily mount the leaves of a butt hinge on the face of a gate, but a neater look is achieved by mounting the leaves on the edge of the gate and the side of the gatepost. When the gate is closed, only the barrel of the hinge will show. If you desire a very tight fit between the post and the gate, recess the leaves into the surfaces of the gate and post with a chisel or router. The recess will also help support the hinge. Because the permissible clearance around a gate is greater than that for a door, recessing the hinge leaves isn't necessary, just a design option.

T-hinges have one rectangular leaf and one long tapered leaf. The rectangular leaf is usually mounted to either the face or the edge of the gatepost, and the long tapered leaf mounts on the face of the gate. T-hinges are the easiest of all hinges to install—just wedge the gate into position, hold the hinge in place, and drive in the screws. When setting the wedges, cock the gate a little toward the gatepost at the top to compensate for the looseness between the hinge's pin and barrel (see the drawing at left). When you remove the wedges, the gate will settle into a level position.

Pintle hinges are very versatile. They can be mounted on round posts as well as on square ones. The pintle is a vertical pin on the end of

An inverted pintle bolt, salvaged from the previous gate, is used here to hang the new gate on a stone pier.

PRO**TIP**

When replacing a gate the old hardware can sometimes be removed. Use a penetrating oil, such as WD-40 to loosen rusty bolts. As a last resort, rusted bolts can be cut free with a hacksaw.

a horizontal bolt. The through-bolt variety has a machine thread, whereas the lag-bolt type has a coarse thread for driving directly into wood. Mounting a pintle on the side of the post lets the gate swing both ways, whereas mounting on the face of the post—called an "overlay" installation—restricts the swing of the gate to one side only. The pintle engages an eye, which is typically formed on the end of a bolt or strap.

Latches There are a few types of gate latches available, from simple to not so simple (see the drawings at right). The typical gate latch consists of a latch bar (or latch pin) and a keeper (or striker). In some versions, the latch bar pivots up and down, settling into a fixed keeper. In other versions the latch pin is fixed and the keeper opens and closes. Mounting either of these is a matter of holding the parts in position, marking the screw holes, and driving the screws.

A slide bolt is similarly straightforward. The bolt slides horizontally, fitting into a keeper or sleeve. A pivot-type latch has an advantage over a slide bolt because it latches itself when shut, whereas a slide bolt requires locking and unlocking. Pivot-type latches also have some built-in

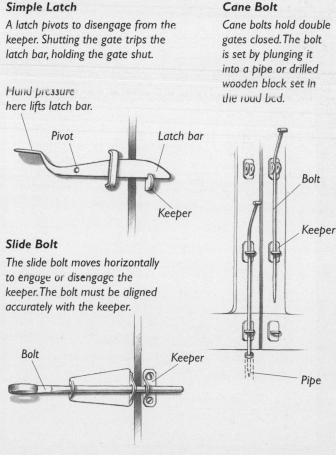

COMMON GATE LATCHES

Simple Latch
A latch pivots to disengage from the keeper. Shutting the gate trips the latch bar, holding the gate shut.

Hand pressure here lifts latch bar.

Pivot   Latch bar

Keeper

Slide Bolt
The slide bolt moves horizontally to engage or disengage the keeper. The bolt must be aligned accurately with the keeper.

Bolt   Keeper

Cane Bolt
Cane bolts hold double gates closed. The bolt is set by plunging it into a pipe or drilled wooden block set in the road bed.

Bolt

Keeper

Pipe

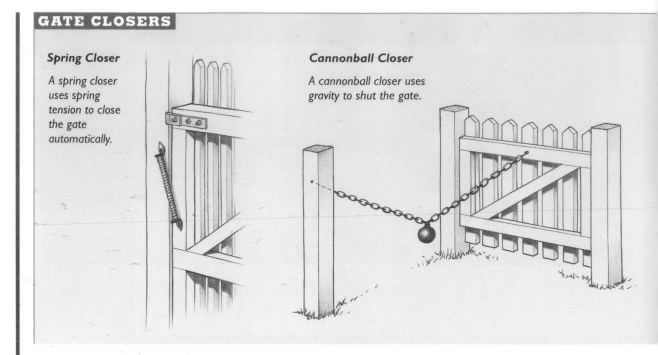

GATE CLOSERS

Spring Closer

A spring closer uses spring tension to close the gate automatically.

Cannonball Closer

A cannonball closer uses gravity to shut the gate.

WHAT CAN GO WRONG

The look of raw galvanized hardware can be improved by painting, but wait a year before doing so. Galvanized structures don't hold paint unless they weather first.

tolerance for misalignment should the gate sag, whereas slide bolts do not.

A cane bolt is used to hold double gates in position, such as in the middle of a driveway. The bolt slides into a pipe or a block of wood set flush in the road bed. Both halves of the gate can be fixed with cane bolts, or one half can be latched to the other (cane-bolted) half.

A mortise latch has a mechanism that's recessed into the edge of the gate stile. Mounting a mortise latch is considerably more work than mounting any kind of surface-mounted latch, but the result is a very neat look.

There are also some very simple ways of latching a gate that don't require much hardware or effort. A bail is a semicircular band, cord, or wire that flips over the top of a gatepost to capture a gate stile or picket. A chain and clip does much the same thing. The chain is fastened to the gatepost, loops around the gate somehow, and its end is then clipped or hooked onto an eye set on the post. These retainers are very forgiving of misalignment, so they're often used for rough

agricultural gates. The hook and eye is another device that isn't too fussy about the gate's fit. A hook hung on the gate slips into an eye set on the post (or vice versa). One type of heavy-duty hook has a spring-loaded jaw that must be retracted for the hook to release from the eye.

Closers A gate that closes by itself is desirable when kids or pets are forbidden to pass (see the drawings above). The spring-loaded butt hinges made for screen doors work fine for small gates. You can also find a heavy-duty spring closer that straddles the hinge stile and gatepost. Perhaps the classiest member of this category is the cannonball closer, which hails from Colonial Williamsburg.

Building a Framed Gate

The pickets in the gate we're constructing are nailed to a sturdy 2×4 frame (see the top photo on the facing page). You can achieve a lighter gate simply by screwing the pickets to a set of cleats. The tops of the pickets are arranged here

This simple framed gate shouts "Enter here!"

in a shieldlike design that's reminiscent of a gothic arch. A similar shape is used to detail the pickets themselves. To simplify the design, you could use spear-point pickets topped straight across, but it's easy to build as is. Another decorative feature of this gate is the asymmetrical arrangement of the braces. There are three braces instead of the typical one or two, which adds strength as well as a chevron motif.

1. Assemble a rectangular frame of 2×4s with screws, as shown in **A**. You can use pipe clamps to hold the pieces together during assembly.

2. Check corner-to-corner measurements to make sure that the frame is square, then scribe a corner brace to fit its intended location. Screw corner braces into the frame, as shown in **B**. Check the frame for square one more time before installing pickets.

3. Nail oversize pickets to the frame, as shown in **C**.

4. Use a trammel stick to scribe a pair of wide arcs that intersect at the top of the middle picket, as shown in **D**. You'll have to find the

length of the trammel and the correct center points by trial and error.

5. Use a template to mark the tops of the pickets. Hold the point of the template to the previously scribed arcs, as shown in **E**.

6. Use a jigsaw to trim the pickets to shape, as shown in **F**.

7. To hang the gate, first prop it in position with temporary blocks or tapered shims. To determine the best-looking arrangement of the

G

The internet is a great way to shop for good-looking gate hardware, since hardware is easily shipped.

When using pressure-treated lumber for gates it's best to use stainless steel fasteners.

hinges, just eyeball them at arm's length, or better yet have a helper move them around so you can regard the composition from a distance.

To install a face-mounted butt hinge or a T-hinge, hold it in position and drive one screw through the hinge into the gate and another screw through the hinge into the post. Leave the other hinge-holes undrilled for now to make adjustments easier. Repeat for the other hinge, and then remove the temporary blocking. If the gate hangs correctly you can install the remaining screws. If an adjustment is necessary, remove one of the screws driven initially, shift the gate slightly relative to the post, and redrive the screw through one of the previously undrilled hinge-holes. When the fit is right drill through all the hinge holes and drive all the screws.

To mount butt hinges on the side of a gate you'll need to support the gate in an open position while you drive the screws. This can be done by shimming the gate with blocks, or with the aid of an assistant. Use the same one-screw-only trick to make adjustments easier.

If you're hanging the gate on pintle hinges, hold the pintle and it's mating eye in position and mark centerlines onto the gate and gatepost. You may need to transfer these marks to the edge of the gate and to the side of the post, depending on whether the gate swings between the posts or overlays the posts. Drill holes and drive the pintles and eyes. Hang the gate and adjust if necessary, either by backing out a lag-threaded shank or by adjusting the jam nuts on a machine-threaded shank, as shown in **G**.

DESIGN
OPTIONS

▲ The well-braced substructure of this gate is covered with narrow saplings—a smart blend of whimsical styling and hard-headed engineering. A pintle hinge marries the gate to a granite pier.

▶ The no-nonsense design of this wooden gate fits well with the crisp masonry surrounding it.

◀ The scrollsawn pickets of this gate are unmistakably Victorian. The gate is divided into halves, making the two resulting panels light and easy to swing.

▲ An air of mystery is created by the partial transparency of this slender gate.

▼ A formally arranged garden with rustic gates of unpeeled logs—a surprising mixed metaphor that succeeds.

ARBORS, PERGOLAS, AND TRELLISES

The use of lightweight wooden skeletons to support climbing plants is as old as agriculture. Although the leafy finery that adorns an arbor, pergola, or trellis is like icing on a cake, the best structures possess a certain beauty in their own right. They achieve this by the artful arrangement of slender parts in regular patterns.

One hoped-for result of this arrangement is a lively sense of visual rhythm. Another sought-after effect is symmetry. Both of these qualities are inherently pleasing, and they acquire even greater drama when set against the asymmetry of nature. Considering the small investment of labor and material they require, arbors, pergolas, and trellises deliver more visual "bang for the buck" than just about any other home project.

In this chapter we'll address some general construction steps that apply to all three types of structures to give you a good base of knowledge. Then we'll show you step by step how to build each type. ▶ ▶ ▶

127

Construction Basics

The structures described in this chapter are open frameworks. There's space between the individual members, but they act in unison, like dancers in a chorus. To help you direct this chorus effectively, I'll start with some guidelines for building framed structures in general, and then look at specific instructions for each structure type— "dance steps," if you will—in the latter part of this chapter.

Marking and cutting parts

The first step in framing a skeletal structure is to take a hard, analytical look at the design. Most garden support structures consist of a few basic parts produced in multiples and arranged in regular patterns. List each type of part on paper, along with the quantity and the exact size.

1. Precut all the parts and stack them in neat piles.

2. Before marking or fastening anything together, try arranging the parts loosely into subassemblies. By doing so, you'll understand how the parts fit together and recognize any problems before you're in the middle of construction. For instance, to mock up the side panels for an arbor, lay two posts on the ground and spread a set of cross members across the posts in their approximate locations. Do the same for the roof assembly.

3. Once the general scheme of things has been rehearsed, it's time to mark the precise spacing of individual members. It's much quicker and more accurate to perform this marking simultaneously on groups of parts rather than marking each piece after it's been installed.

Begin the marking process with the main posts. Nestle a group of posts together side by side with their ends carefully lined up (see the drawing below). Then mark cross-member

LAYING OUT POSTS FOR A PERGOLA

Lay out all four posts at the same time. Using the working drawing as a guide, make a layout stick with six key measurements. Transfer these measurements to the posts before cutting and assembly begins. A seventh measurement on the rod for grade is only approximate. The actual grade will vary.

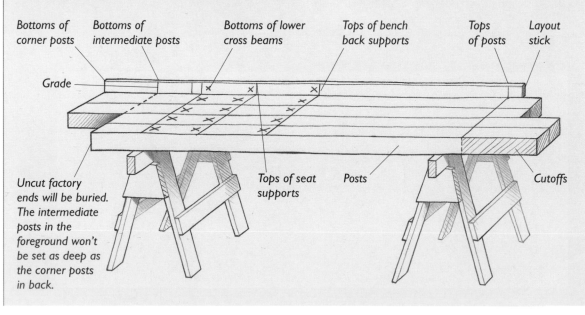

Bottoms of corner posts

Bottoms of intermediate posts

Bottoms of lower cross beams

Tops of bench back supports

Tops of posts

Layout stick

Grade

Uncut factory ends will be buried. The intermediate posts in the foreground won't be set as deep as the corner posts in back.

Tops of seat supports

Posts

Cutoffs

What's the Difference?

THE TERMS TRELLIS, ARBOR, AND PERGOLA are often used interchangeably, depending on whom you talk to. The problem of labels is exacerbated by the amazing variety of structures and the gardens they adorn. The following definitions are offered for the purposes of this book, although the distinctions put forth here are often blurred in practice.

A trellis is a light framework used to support a vine or a climbing shrub. Though a trellis is often fastened to a building for support, other types are freestanding, such as those used in a vegetable garden to support cucumbers and tomatoes. A trellis should be strong enough to support a sopping wet vine in full leaf, yet delicate enough to blend gracefully with a winter landscape.

An arbor is an effective way of announcing a transition from one space, such as the street, to another space, such as the front yard. Although the skeletal form of a well-executed arbor needs no further adornment, an arbor is often used to support flowering vines and shrubs. The thicker the greenery that encompasses the arbor, the greater the sense of mystery about what lies beyond it.

A pergola is a more substantial cousin of the arbor. As such, it can stand on its own in a remote part of the landscape or be as close as a backyard patio. Whereas an arbor serves as a passageway, a pergola is more of an outdoor room. It often contains seating, which encourages people to pause and take in the view. The pergola also acts as an important focal point when viewed from a distance.

This trellis helps support a climbing shrub as it scales a brick wall.

An arbor delicately punctuates the transition from street to front yard. Notice how its subtle arch rhymes with the decorative tracery over the front porch.

The regular spacing of the roof poles on this simple pergola sets up a pleasing visual rhythm.

locations on one of the posts. (You can even wait until this point to mark the overall length of the posts, rather than measuring each one individually.) Do your measuring with a tape measure, or prepare a special layout stick with only the necessary measurements on it. As a way of working out details in advance, builders and cabinetmakers like to develop a complete set of layout sticks (one for height, one for breadth, and one for width) before a single piece of wood is cut.

4. After establishing cross-member locations on one of the posts, use a square to extend the marks onto all the posts in the group. You can mark where both edges of the cross member will go, but laying out just one edge is all that's really necessary. Just make sure you mark an X to show which side of the line the cross member will go on. After marking the posts, mark the other members as sets as well.

5. When the parts are ready, lay out the structure's footprint and assemble the parts into as large a unit as you can comfortably erect. How

big the unit is may depend on the number (and size) of your helpers. A small arbor might be fully assembled before installation, whereas a convenient subassembly for a pergola might consist of just two posts and a cross beam.

Building wooden arches

An important subassembly in many garden projects is the arch. A shallow arch can be cut from a single wide board (see the photo below). A deep arch can be cut from a sheet of plywood, but plywood doesn't hold up well outdoors, especially with its edges exposed. A better solution for a deep arch is to join several pieces of solid lumber together by using a technique called bricklaying. In bricklaying, individual curved segments are stacked with their ends staggered to create an overlap—sort of like laying bricks (see the left drawing on the facing page).

1. To make templates for the overlapping arch segments, first lay out the arch full scale on a sheet of ¼-in. plywood, then divide it into thirds. A large arch may need to be divided

The shallow arches of this arbor were sawn from wide redwood boards.

COMPOSING A BRICK-LAID ARCH

Each arch requires two outer layers and one middle layer. Total pieces required for job: 16 segment pieces and 4 dogleg pieces. (Each arbor requires two arches.)

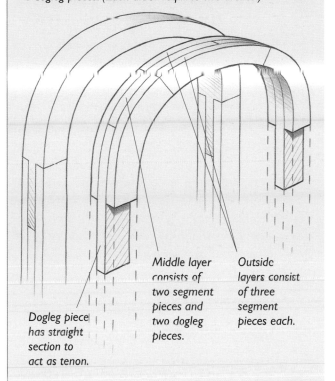

Dogleg piece has straight section to act as tenon.

Middle layer consists of two segment pieces and two dogleg pieces.

Outside layers consist of three segment pieces each.

LAYING OUT ARCH SEGMENTS WITH A TRAMMEL STICK

Step 1
Set the nail in the trammel stick at A (center of arch). Use pencil holes 1 and 2 (outside and inside radii) to draw the arch.

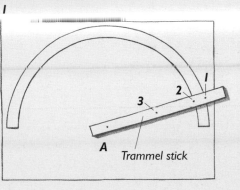

1

Trammel stick

Step 2
Set the center nail at B on the outside circumference. Use the line made by pencil hole 1 (outside radius) to divide the outside circumference into a 1/3 segment, crossing the circumference at C. Repeat on the other side, with center 1 at D and crossing at E.

Step 3
Connect C and E to center point A, thus dividing the arch into three equal segments.

2 & 3

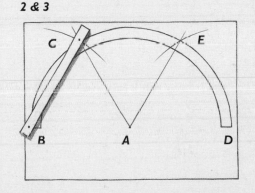

Step 4
Using D and E as center points and an arbitrary distance as a radius (pencil hole 3), swing overlapping arcs.

Step 5
Connect the center of arch A to the point where arcs overlap, thus dividing a 1/3 segment into two 1/6 segments.

4, 5 & 6

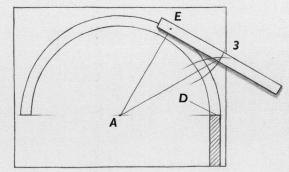

Step 6
Extend the arch with straight lines to form a tenon. This makes the dogleg piece.

into more than three segments, whereas a small arch might be built up from just two. The wider the boards you have to work with, the fewer segments will be required.

To lay out the curve of the arch, use a trammel stick—a sort of overgrown compass (see the photo **D** on p. 122). A nail protrudes through the stick at one end to act as a center point, and the other end has holes drilled at different locations to receive a pencil.

You can also use the trammel stick to divide the arch into segments (see the drawings at right). The basic geometry is as follows: When the radius of a circle is "stepped off" along the circle's circumference three times, the distance traveled will equal one half of the circle, or the arch.

ATTACHING POSTS TO THE ARCH

Straight 1×4s layered together to make posts

Tenon added to 1/6 segment of arch to interlock with post

Edge view of arch

Use only clear lumber (without knots) for building arches. Knots cause weak points that can ruin all your hard work.

TRADE SECRET

Arch segments are prone to splitting because their grain runs diagonally across the segment at each end, a condition known as short grain. To keep the short grain from splitting, be sure to drill pilot holes for nails or screws.

2. After laying out and dividing the arch on plywood, cut the segments out and use them as templates. In addition to one-third segments, one-sixth segments will be required at both ends of the arch to create an offset in one of the layers, in the same way that a half brick is used in every other course of a brick wall. In the example shown in the drawing above, a straight section has been added to the one-sixth segment to form a tenon (or tongue) that will interlock with the post of the arbor. This extended segment is called a "dogleg" because of its crooked shape.

3. Place the templates on the workpieces and trace them. Then cut out the pieces with a jigsaw or bandsaw.

4. To assemble the arch, start by layering a one-sixth segment onto a one-third segment, keeping the edges carefully aligned. Add another one-third segment next, and so on, until the arch is complete. The process is sort of like leap-frogging. A combination of glue and screws works well for laminating the pieces.

Leveling post holes

After putting together the assembly (or subassemblies), check the as-built distance between posts against the footprint layout you did on the ground. If the measurements check out, go ahead and dig your holes. If not, adjust the footprint accordingly.

The bottoms of your post holes must be level with each other or the structure will not stand straight. The question is how to gauge the depth of the holes in relation to each other, because a spirit level can't be placed directly between the bottoms of the holes. Knowing the depth of the holes below grade isn't much help because the grade itself is almost always out of level. So to check for level, builders use an optical instrument with a telescope and a special calibrated rod.

Fortunately, most garden structures are compact, which allows you to use a simple method for gauging the depth of post holes.

1. Start by setting a stake somewhere in the middle of the footprint as an arbitrary benchmark (see the drawing on the facing page). Drive the stake with a sledgehammer until it feels good and solid. If the top of the stake slopes much in any direction, saw it off to produce a fairly level surface.

The top of a stake serves as an arbitrary benchmark. By measuring the depth of each hole in relation to the stake, the bottoms of the holes can be leveled with each other.

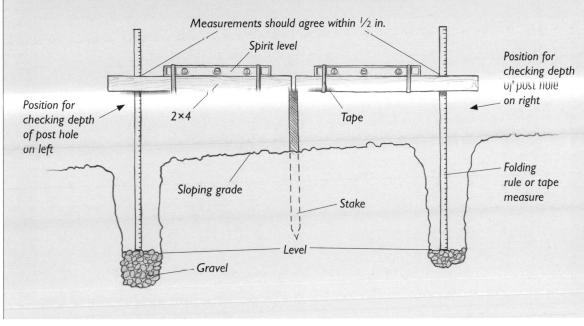

Measurements should agree within ½ in.

Spirit level

2×4

Position for checking depth of post hole on left

Tape

Position for checking depth of post hole on right

Sloping grade

Stake

Level

Gravel

Folding rule or tape measure

The price of laser levels has come within reach of homeowners (about $100). If you do many outdoor projects, these instruments will come in handy.

2. Now find a straightedge long enough to reach horizontally from the stake to each hole (a straight 2×4 will do nicely). Tape your spirit level to the straightedge. (If your level is long enough by itself, you won't need the straightedge.)

Rest one end of the straightedge on the stake and hold the other end against a folding rule or tape measure held vertically in the hole. Move the free end of the straightedge up or down until the bubble in the level reads true, and then see where the top of the straightedge crosses the ruler. Write down the measurement. Now do the same thing with the other post holes and compare the measurements.

3. Add a few inches of gravel to each hole for drainage, adding somewhat more to the deepest holes and somewhat less to the shallower holes. Check the measurements again, and adjust the depths with more gravel as necessary. Don't go

crazy. If you get all the measurements within ½ in., you're okay. After raising the structure into position, you can fine-tune the alignment by beating on the tops of too-high posts with a sledgehammer (be sure to use a block of wood as a cushion to prevent damage to the post).

Tying, bracing, and backfilling

A large structure such as a pergola is best raised in two half sections, with each section consisting of two posts and a primary cross member (see the top drawing on p. 134). After raising both half sections, tie them together with secondary cross members going perpendicular to the primary cross members. All sorts of cross-member arrangements are possible, which can make carpentry nomenclature rather subjective. The underlying idea, however, is that one set of cross members supports a second set oriented perpendicular to the first.

Keep your knees bent and your back straight when lifting heavy frames.

TYING AND BRACING POSTS

Step 1
When the half sections are raised, the posts are nonparallel and out of plumb.

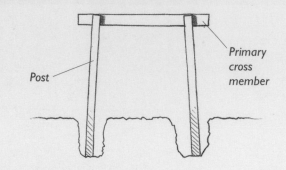

Post

Primary cross member

Step 2
Tack a temporary horizontal batten in place just above grade so that the posts are parallel, although they may still be out of plumb (racked).

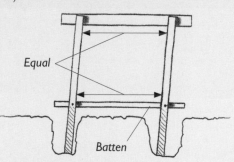

Equal

Batten

Step 3
Attach diagonal braces to the structure to ensure that the posts are parallel and plumb and ready for backfill.

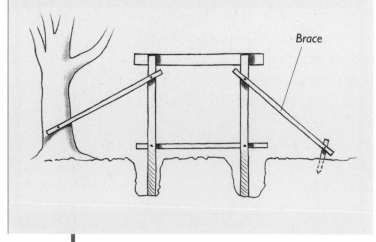

Brace

When both sets of cross members are in place, the overall dimensions of the structure will be locked in at the tops of the posts, but the bottoms are still free to move around. Solve this by tacking temporary horizontal battens just above grade to hold the bottoms of the posts the correct distance apart during backfilling (see the middle drawing at left). Before installing the battens, mark on each end the correct post-to-post distance. (This distance can be read off the plans or simply transferred from the top of the assembly, where the posts are already joined together by cross members.)

When the bottoms of the posts are held together properly, the posts will all be parallel, but they may still be tilted out of plumb. This effect is called racking. To ensure that the posts remain truly plumb (vertical) while the backfilling is completed, the structure must be braced diagonally (see the bottom drawing at left).

1. Drive stakes in the ground a few feet from each corner.

2. Nail a temporary diagonal brace from each stake to the top of its corresponding post to stiffen the structure and hold it plumb. You'll need to gauge the plumbness of the post with a level as you nail the brace. If it's out of plumb, have a helper lean on the post as you drive a nail through the brace into the post.

3. Backfill all the holes (for more on backfilling posts, see p. 37). Once all the holes have been backfilled, remove the diagonal braces and temporary horizontal battens—the earth will hold the posts upright.

The posts and arches for this rose arbor are constructed by sandwiching three layers of cedar boards. Leaving intermittent voids in the middle layer adds to the light, airy feeling of the design.

Completing the skeleton

Once the basic framework of a structure has been erected, additional parts are usually added as infill. These parts can be attached in different ways, but nailing is the simplest.

Fasten the parts to each other, being sure to mark them with the correct spacing beforehand. A part may bow inward or outward, but lining it up with the correct marks on the adjoining part will straighten it. Some persuasion may be necessary. Press on the offending part with a hand or foot as the adjoining part is being nailed on, or pry it into position.

Building an Arbor

This arched arbor is a classic (see the photo above). The arch makes this one of the more challenging projects in the book, but if you take it one step at a time, it will be manageable. The geometry of the circle is actually fairly simple, which makes this circular arch a lot less troublesome than elliptical versions. If you're nervous about the arch, you can do a square-top arbor instead. The look would be similar to the top of a basic pergola.

The arch and posts of this arbor are built up by layering thin boards together, which simpli-

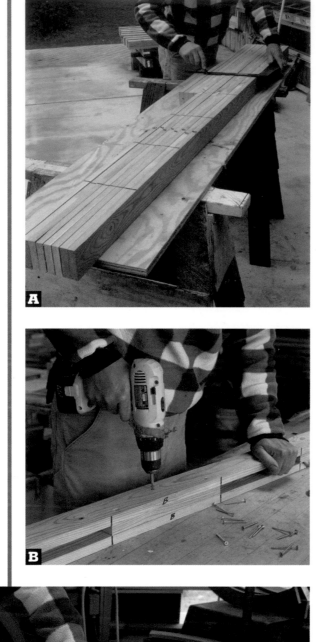

fies the joinery. For instance, by extending the middle layer of the arch, a tenon is produced so you don't have to saw this joint separately from a thick piece (see the drawing on p. 132). Portions of the middle layer have been left out of the posts to give the structure an airy feeling.

To increase the diameter of the arch, you'll need wider boards and perhaps a greater number of segments making up the curve. When upsizing, you might also consider using three layers of 5/4 lumber instead of the 1× shown here to maintain the proper scale.

1. Rack up 1×4s for posts side by side for marking, along with filler blocks. Use a framing square to mark all the pieces at once, as shown in **A**.

2. To make each post, assemble a pair of 1×4s with blocks in between. The open space left between the blocks gives the arbor a light appearance. The letter B written on the outer layers indicates the location of a block, as shown in **B**.

3. Lay out the arch on a sheet of plywood, using a trammel stick to draw the inner and outer curves, as shown in **C** (see the drawings on p. 131 for more on using a trammel stick). Divide the arch into segments (in this case thirds) and then cut individual templates out of the plywood. You'll need a plain template representing one full segment and a "dogleg" template, which represents a half segment with a straight extension to form a tenon. Tenons will connect the arches to their respective posts.

4. Trace the dogleg template onto a blank of cedar and mark the spring line for the arch, as shown in **D**. The spring line is where the end

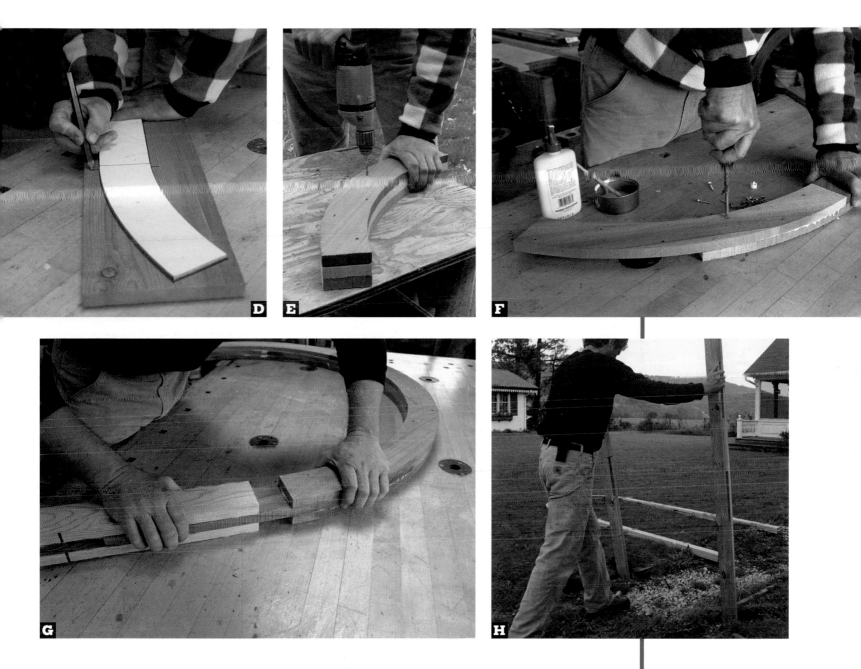

of the first segment piece will be positioned when the lamination process begins. Cut out the piece with a jigsaw. Trace and cut out the plain segments of the arch as well.

5. Drill clearance holes in the segment pieces so that they don't split when they are screwed. To speed things up, drill three pieces at a time, as shown in **E**.

6. Laminate the segment pieces together using galvanized screws and waterproof glue, as shown in **F**.

7. Attach the arch to the post by slipping the straight portion of the dogleg piece between 1×4s, as shown in **G**.

8. Set the arch/post assembly in the post holes, as shown in **H**.

9. After marking the post locations on the crosspieces, screw them to the posts, as shown in **I**.

10. Plumb the posts, then install some temporary bracing. After bracing the arbor, backfill the post holes, as shown in **J**.

11. Attach additional cross pieces at the arch, as shown in **K**.

This pergola marks the transition from a front yard to a backyard. Vines will soon enclose the structure, creating a shady place to sit while helping to screen off the backyard from street traffic. The diagonal lattice panels were cut from commercially available 4 ft. by 8 ft. lattice units.

PRO TIP

If you don't want lattice, consider providing some sort of temporary ladder to assist small vines as they grow up the posts. This can be wire netting, strings, or a series of nails or dowels set partway into the posts. When the vine has established itself, the temporary support can be removed.

Building a Pergola with Seats

This pergola with seats and lattice panels is a nice variation of the basic form. The seats add a functional aspect, as does the lattice, which vines can easily grow on.

The "roof" of a pergola can be a simple set of rafters going in one direction, or you can add purlins at right angles to the rafters to produce the crisscross pattern shown here. Curved details like the scalloped seat slats and the scrolled ends

of the rafters give the pergola a graceful look. These cuts are easy to make with a jigsaw. If you don't have a jigsaw, you can still produce decorative effects by pointing or beveling the various members with straight cuts. For instance, the lower corner of each rafter can be chopped off at a 45-degree angle instead of scroll cutting.

For a more traditional and open pergola, you could omit the lattice panels and the seats. In that case you won't need the intermediate posts either—just the four corner posts.

shown in **A**. Once the holes are marked, you can dig them.

2. After crosscutting the rafters to length, trim their ends with a jigsaw, as shown in **B**. Use a plywood template to outline this decorative cut.

3. Line up the rafters side by side, then lay out the purlin locations on the rafters' top edges, as shown in **C**.

4. Mark header locations (left) on the undersides of the two intermediate rafters, as shown in **D**. Mark post locations (right) on the undersides of the two outer rafters.

5. Cut the 4×4 posts to length (see the drawing on p. 128), then screw each outside rafter to a pair of posts, as shown in **E**.

6. Raise the first post/rafter assembly into position, as shown in **F**. Once this one is up, you can raise the next one.

7. Install a header to tie the two post/rafter assemblies together at the top, as shown in **G**. Then install a seat ledger to tie the two post/rafter assemblies together at the bottom.

1. Lay out the structure's footprint with stringlines or a plywood template. Then simulate the location of a 4×4 post relative to the footprint by placing a 4×4 block just inside the layout lines. Spray-paint around the block to lay out the surrounding post hole, as

8. Tack temporary battens on the long sides to hold the bottoms of the posts the correct distance apart, then install temporary diagonal bracing to hold the structure plumb. After the bracing is installed, backfill and tamp the holes, as shown in **H**.

9. Attach intermediate posts against the outside rafters with screws, then install permanent corner braces for extra rigidity, as shown in **I**.

10. Nail diagonal lattice panels onto the framing, as shown in **J**.

11. Toenail intermediate rafters onto the headers, lay out the rafter locations on the purlins, then nail the purlins onto the rafters, as shown in **K**. Crooked rafters may have to be pushed into position to line up correctly with the marks on the purlins.

12. Make the back of the seat with decorative slats, as shown in **L**.

Siting a Pergola

THE VIEWS THROUGH

within a pergola are special. To exploit this dramatic potential fully, a pergola should be situated carefully. Site the structure to take advantage of any potential focal points, such as a sundial or a special tree. After picking a likely location, construct a simple mockup. Drive poles or saplings at the corners, and then stand back for a look. From inside the mockup, try to visualize each view during each season. Move the poles around until you've found the best position.

The pergola in this yard is carefully situated to draw the eye to a topiary arch beyond.

Building a Trellis with Planter

This trellis with a planter is attractive, freestanding, and moveable. It's easy to build, and you can modify the design to suit your needs. For instance, you can downsize the planter to produce a window box, or you can build the trellis by itself to put up against your house. Cutouts in the latticework can produce interesting "windows" for vines to grow around. To impart a rustic look, use saplings for the trellis instead of lumber. Coping and molding around the edge of the planter give it a finished look, but they might be out of place on a naturalized version.

Standard 1× boards are fine for the trellis, but you'll need thicker boards to hold the earth in place in the planter. This planter is made with 5/4 boards, but a wider 4-ft. version would require 2× lumber for strength.

Notice that the grain on the planter's end boards runs vertically. This is important, because screws driven into the edge of a board will hold securely; screws driven into end grain will not. If the end boards were positioned horizontally, the screws holding the front and back would be going into end grain. Eventually, the screws would pull out.

This freestanding planter with an attached trellis would be suitable for a deck or patio. A molded coping around the planter adds a touch of class. To render the same design in a rustic version, you could use roughsawn lumber for the planter and crossed saplings for the trellis.

1. Predrill the side boards to avoid splitting them when they are screwed. Drilling three at once saves time, as shown in **A**.

2. Trim away part of the lowermost side board, leaving a short, uncut section at both ends, as shown in **B**. This forms little legs at the four corners to keep the planter from tipping and to promote drainage.

3. Screw the side boards to the 2×12 end boards, as shown in **C**.

4. Nail the 2×12 bottom board in place, then drill drainage holes in it, as shown in **D**.

5. Rip the 2½-in.-wide copings on a tablesaw and miter the ends with a hand miter box or a chopsaw. You can also cut the miter joint with

a circular saw, retracting the blade guard with your thumb to keep it from binding, as shown in **E**. Retracting the blade guard isn't necessary with square cuts.

6. Nail the copings to the top edges of the planter. Keep the miter joint aligned with a C-clamp, then use finish nails to fasten the joint permanently, as shown in **F**.

7. Miter one end of a molding, then hold the piece in position and mark the other end, as shown in **G**.

8. Cut the miter joint on a hand miter box or with a chopsaw, as shown in **H**.

9. Mark the trellis's vertical pieces to show the locations of the horizontal pieces, as shown in **I**. Use a bar clamp to hold the pieces in align-

ment for marking. Mark the horizontals in the same way to show the location of the verticals.

10. Transfer layout marks from one of the horizontal pieces to the back of the planter, as shown in **J**.

11. Screw vertical pieces for the trellis to the back of the planter, as shown in **K**.

12. Fasten the cross pieces to the vertical pieces with finish nails, as shown in **L**. Then drive screws in from the back to reinforce the overlaps.

DESIGN
OPTIONS

▲ This Craftsman-style pergola is both part of the house and part of the landscape.

▶ The construction of this arbor is nothing fancy, but a robust clematis vine makes it sing.

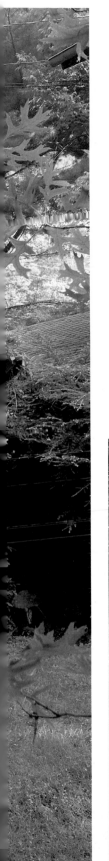

The strong symmetry of this trellis extends right down to the clasped hands of the angel in the center. Swirling around this peaceful center is a raucous wisteria vine.

▲ This elegant trellis was constructed with whips (slender branches) garnered from an apple orchard in springtime.

◄ The Eastlake styling of this covered bench is complemented by a profusion of climbing roses.

GAZEBOS

Gazebos are the most advanced structures in this book. They are essentially little houses, with a floor and a roof just like a home. In fact, the carpentry required for a gazebo can be more advanced than house carpentry when the gazebo is an octagonal or hexagonal shape. The level of difficulty also depends on the overall style of the gazebo, its size, the type of roof you install, and the details you add, like railings and screens.

Before tackling a gazebo you may want to consult other books in the Build Like a Pro series that focus on framing, trim, and roofing. By sharpening these skills you can build a gazebo that fits your landscape better than a prefab unit. ▶ ▶ ▶

This perky gazebo has a personality of its own, sporting keystone arches and a conical roof. It takes its cues from a nearby home, which features similar detailing and materials.

Gazebo Design

Gazebos come in all shapes and sizes. Choose the style that best matches your home and landscape, then move on to other decisions. Size will be a matter of balancing the gazebo's intended use with your budget and ability. The shape of your gazebo depends on such factors as the number of sides, the steepness of the roof, and the style of the cornice (overhang). Details, such as flooring and railings, will flesh out the design.

Size and shape

A typical size for a gazebo is 10 ft. in diameter. This will hold two chairs and a small table comfortably, and the project will be manageable for two people. Larger gazebos can accommodate

family gatherings, but as the diameter increases the floor and roof areas increase exponentially and some serious foundations will be required under the posts. A gazebo smaller than 10 ft. might serve as a landscape ornament, but it would feel cramped with more than a single occupant.

Square gazebos are sometimes seen, but most gazebos have more than four sides. Octagonal gazebos are the norm, but the hexagon has some advantages over its eight-sided cousin. Practically speaking, the six-sided hexagon requires two less of everything—posts, rails, headers, and so on. Aesthetically, the hexagon is more angular than the almost-round octagon, so the corners have more visual punch. Finally, the hexagon shape is very easy to lay out, whether it's for the joints of a round arch or for the plan of a gazebo.

Roof design

A gazebo is mostly roof, so the roof design will dictate cost and complexity more than any other decision. You'll need to consider shape, steepness, type of roof covering, and whether or not to include a cupola.

Most gazebo roofs are hipped, meaning the intersecting roof planes form ridges called "hips." Hip roofs typically feature intersecting roof planes that are flat (meaning not rounded), but some hip roofs have rounded roof profiles, such as on a reverse curve (bell-shaped). These rounded forms are rarely used, however, so the primary design decision for most gazebo builders is pitch, or how steep to make the roof.

Your choice of roof pitch has practical consequences as well as aesthetic ones. Steep roofs shed water better than low-pitch roofs, so they're required for decay-sensitive roof coverings such as wood shingles. Asphalt shingles require a minimum pitch of 3 in. per foot to

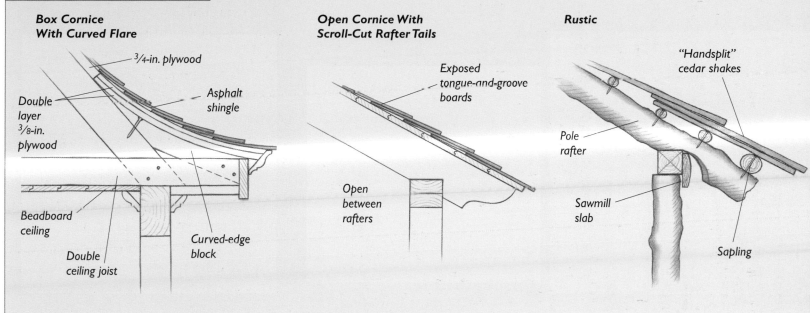

Box Cornice With Curved Flare

3/4-in. plywood

Asphalt shingle

Double layer 3/8-in. plywood

Beadboard ceiling

Double ceiling joist

Curved-edge block

Open Cornice With Scroll-Cut Rafter Tails

Exposed tongue-and-groove boards

Open between rafters

Rustic

"Handsplit" cedar shakes

Pole rafter

Sawmill slab

Sapling

shed water effectively. Low-pitch roofs do have some advantages: They require less material to build, and they're easy to work on because you can stand on a low-pitch roof without scaffolding. To make a low-pitch roof look taller, you can add a cupola.

The intersection of a roof with the sides of a structure is called the cornice. A formal gazebo will have an enclosed cornice, sometimes referred to as a box cornice. In this style of cornice the rafter tails (the lower ends of the roof beams) are concealed. Victorian and rustic styles have exposed rafter tails that can be left plain or worked into fancy shapes.

The underside of a gazebo roof can be left exposed or be concealed by a flat ceiling. Exposed roof framing is attractive if the workmanship is good. If the roof framing is crude, a flat ceiling gives a more finished appearance. A flat ceiling will also prevent birds, bats, and insects from making nests inside. Beadboard is an attractive choice for ceilings. You can use either

Roof Pitch

PITCH IS USUALLY MEASURED in inches per foot, rather than degrees. For instance, a roof with a 45-degree slope is said to have a 12-in.-per-foot pitch. That means that for every 1 ft. of horizontal distance the roof travels it will rise 12 in. Knowing the pitch allows you to quickly calculate the overall rise, or height, of the roof based on its "run," or horizontal travel. For instance, a gazebo with a 10-ft. diameter will be spanned by two opposing roof surfaces, each of which will travel 5 ft. horizontally from the outside to the center. If these roof surfaces have a pitch of 6-in.-per-foot, they will rise 30 in. overall (6 in. × 5 = 30 in.).

the genuine tongue-and-groove variety or a look-alike sheet product.

Gazebo floors can be masonry, wood, or a wood substitute. Masonry is the most durable, but also the most work. Wood is fast and easy, but susceptible to wear and tear. The new synthetic deck boards offer a good compromise—the workability of wood with some of the durability of masonry.

A masonry floor requires a concrete slab to be poured around the posts of the gazebo. Temporary form boards are screwed to the posts to contain the wet concrete. The forms should be well braced or they may bow outward during the pour. A 4-in. layer of gravel is laid on the ground for good drainage, and wire reinforcing mesh is laid over the gravel. The mesh should be propped up 1 in. or 2 in. so that it becomes fully embedded in concrete during the pour. The slab can be troweled smooth to provide a finished surface, in which case dye can be used to color the concrete.

MASONRY FLOOR SECTION

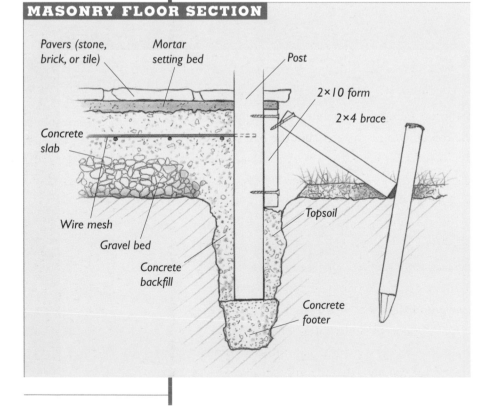

- Pavers (stone, brick, or tile)
- Mortar setting bed
- Post
- 2×10 form
- 2×4 brace
- Concrete slab
- Wire mesh
- Gravel bed
- Concrete backfill
- Topsoil
- Concrete footer

Avoiding a Tilt

GAZEBOS DON'T HAVE SOLID WALLS to provide lateral stiffness, so a poorly built gazebo can easily tilt. Built-in seating will help to buttress the posts of a gazebo. Railings that have any kind of diagonal configuration will also brace a gazebo from side to side, but a railing with vertical spindles won't. The only way to achieve lateral stiffness without diagonal railings or built-in seating is to plant the posts of a gazebo deeply in the ground.

The posts supporting this gazebo don't extend into the ground. As a result, the structure has tilted sideways.

If stone, brick, or tile pavers are to be applied over the concrete, the slab should be left rough.

Wood decking for a gazebo should be spaced to let water drain through the cracks. However, if the deck boards have a high moisture content they can be laid tightly together and gaps will appear later as the boards shrink. Pressure-treated decking is the standard, but cedar and redwood are more refined—and more expensive—options. Cedar and redwood can be nailed down because

Built-in seating and ample proportions make this rustic gazebo an inviting venue for summer gatherings.

TRADE SECRET

Synthetic decking has more decay resistance and stability than wood. Synthetics are not as stiff as wood, however, so they cannot span as great a distance. Wood decking can span 16 in. for a 1-in. board thickness, and 24 in. or more for heavier thicknesses. If you use synthetic decking instead of wood, be sure to check the manufacturer's recommendations for maximum span between floor joists (beams). If you exceed the recommendation your deck boards will feel spongy to walk on and may sag.

they are inherently stable, whereas pressure-treated decking is screwed down to keep it from warping. The new contender is synthetic decking, which now comes in a bewildering array of choices, from wood/plastic composites to all-plastic products such as PVC. Synthetic decking is stable and durable, albeit bland in appearance.

Gazebos usually have railings, although the absence of a railing can impart a temple look that's appropriate in a formal garden. At the high end, railings with heavy turned balusters are appropriate for formal styles such as Georgian. For Colonial Revival, a serviceable railing of straight square spindles will do. Victorian railings can get rather wild, with balusters arranged in non-rectilinear patterns. A country setting invites the use of scrollsawn boards, with the space between the boards representing objects such as hearts or flowers.

Built-in seating can work nicely around the perimeter of a gazebo. The simplest way to make a comfortable seat is to use cushions, but be sure to allow for their thickness in your design. Standard seat height is about 17 in. You can make a comfortable all-wood seat by scrollsawing the seat supports to a bottom-friendly curve, then covering the seats with narrow sanded boards.

Building a Victorian Gazebo

In this chapter, we'll build a hexagonal gazebo featuring a concave roof and a fancy railing (see the top drawing on p. 154), but the basic procedure would be similar even without these refinements. The concentric floorboard design is made possible by the underlying pie-shaped floor framing (see the bottom drawing on p. 154). Although this framing system looks complicated, it actually simplifies matters because it's composed of six triangular subassemblies that are all the same. A conventionally framed floor, on the other hand, would require joists of various lengths with a variety of end cuts. Another advantage of the pie-wedge system is that it automatically locks all

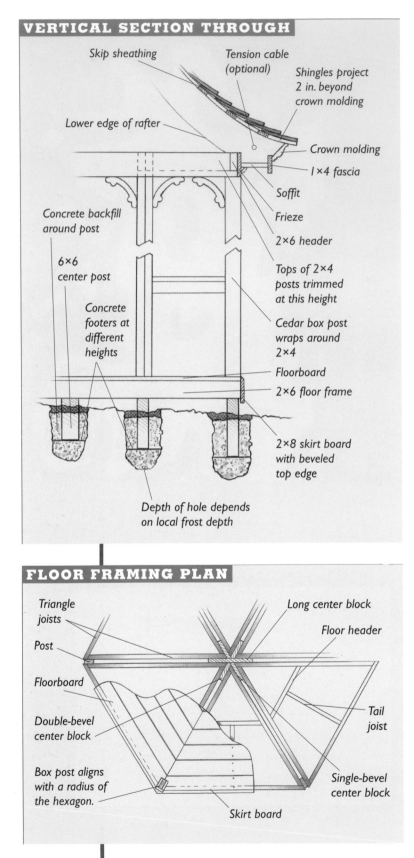

VERTICAL SECTION THROUGH

Skip sheathing

Tension cable (optional)

Shingles project 2 in. beyond crown molding

Lower edge of rafter

Crown molding

1×4 fascia

Soffit

Frieze

2×6 header

Concrete backfill around post

6×6 center post

Tops of 2×4 posts trimmed at this height

Concrete footers at different heights

Cedar box post wraps around 2×4

Floorboard

2×6 floor frame

2×8 skirt board with beveled top edge

Depth of hole depends on local frost depth

FLOOR FRAMING PLAN

Triangle joists

Long center block

Floor header

Post

Floorboard

Double-bevel center block

Tail joist

Box post aligns with a radius of the hexagon.

Single-bevel center block

Skirt board

the posts in the correct orientation, aligned on a radius of the hexagon.

Layout and posts

The first thing you need to do is establish the location of the gazebo and its posts. Then you'll be ready to dig the post holes.

1. Lay down three sheets of plywood on a wide open floor (such as your garage) and draw a half-plan of the gazebo at full scale on the plywood. Start by drawing a large half circle with a trammel stick (see p. 131) and then use the trammel to step off four points on the half circle to indicate the corner points of a half-hexagon. Then draw in the pie-shaped floor sections, the posts, and so forth. The finished plan will guide you in making cuts on the various floor members by giving you their precise length and orientation. All the end-cuts in this project have an angle of either 60 degrees or 90 degrees (square).

2. At the site, dig a 12-in.-dia. hole at the center of the future gazebo. The depth of the hole should go down to the frost line of your locality. Pour a 4-in.-thick concrete footer in the bottom of the hole, agitating the concrete slightly to level it off. Let the concrete harden overnight, and then bury a length of pressure-treated 6×6 vertically in the hole. The top of the 6×6 will provide a center point for the trammel stick, and it will also remain to provide support to the pie wedges of the floor frame where they converge. The top of the 6×6 should be reasonably level, and it should be just a few inches above grade.

3. Check your plan to determine the radius from the gazebo's centerpoint to the centers

of the posts, and make a trammel stick measuring that dimension. Lay six flat blocks on the ground in the approximate location of the posts, and use the trammel to swing an arc through all six blocks, marking the blocks, as shown in **A**. Starting from the middle of one of the blocks, step off six consecutive arcs from block to block. The intersection of each arc with the circumference line becomes the centerpoint for the next arc, and so forth until you go all the way around the circle. This will precisely indicate the post centers. If the trammel misses any of the blocks, move the block, draw a new arc through it, and step off again from the preceding point.

4. Before you remove the blocks to dig your post holes, you'll need to record the centerlines for each post on the ground. To do this, pull a line from the gazebo centerpoint through each block to another point a few feet outside the digging area. Drive a pin here so you can re-establish this line periodically to check the hole's location and centerpoint as you dig, as shown in **B** (on p. 156). To confirm the

Orientation of Posts

SQUARE CORNER POSTS FIT NEATLY in a square structure, but how should a square post be oriented in a hexagon or octagon? Builders sometimes get into trouble by setting one face of the post flush with a side (see the right drawing below). At first this might appear to simplify matters, but as other framing members and trim elements are added it leads to problems because the angle of intersection varies from one side to the next. I prefer to align posts on radii that go from the center to the corners of the gazebo (see the left drawing below). That way all horizontal members will join the post at the same angle.

CORNER-POST OPTIONS FOR AN OCTAGONAL GAZEBO

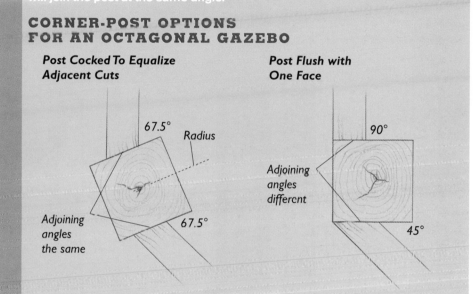

Post Cocked To Equalize Adjacent Cuts

67.5°
Radius
Adjoining angles the same
67.5°

Post Flush with One Face

90°
Adjoining angles different
45°

POST-HOLE LAYOUT

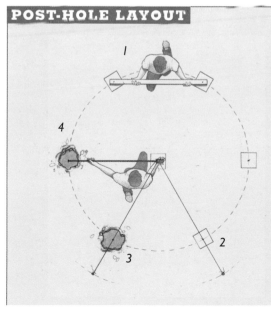

1. Use a trammel stick to locate center points of posts on wood blocks.

2. Pull a line through each center point and drive a pin a few feet beyond the hole location.

3. Use the line as you dig to confirm that the center you marked is still actually in the center of the hole.

4. Check the measurement from the center of the gazebo to the center of the hole.

distance of the hole from the center of the gazebo after the blocks have been removed, simply take a measurement, as shown in **C**.

5. Dig all the post holes to the same depth—namely, the frost-free depth specified by your local building department. Then pour footers at the bottoms of these holes like you did for the center hole.

Because the grade probably varies and the holes are the same depth, the footers won't necessarily be at the same height (see the top drawing on p. 154). That's okay, because later the tops of the posts that stand on these footers will be trimmed even. This scenario is different than the one described for the arbor on p. 133, where the post holes were roughly leveled with gravel and the posts were precut to the same length. Gravel footers can be adjusted in the hole because they're dry, but adjusting wet concrete footers is impractical.

Floor

The 2×4 posts are set in the holes and the preassembled pie-shaped floor sections are attached to them. Connecting blocks tie the pie sections to each other at the center of the floor.

1. Assemble the six triangular floor sections, including the floor headers and tail joists for each section, on a flat surface, as shown in **D**. Geometrically speaking, these are equilateral triangles, so the sides are all identical. Just be sure when you assemble them that the butt joints at the corners go in sequence, like a dog chasing its tail (see the bottom drawing on p. 154).

2. Set all the posts in their respective holes. Now mark the height of the floor frame on

the posts using a 2×6 with a level taped to it, stretching it across from the center post to the newly installed posts, as shown in **E**. Strike a mark on each post along the top edge of the 2×6 to show the correct elevation (height) of the floor framing. Then, with the inward-facing corner of a floor section resting on the center post, align the floor section with the floor-height lines you marked on the posts and screw those two corners to the two gazebo posts. Make sure the posts are standing plumb before you drive in all the screws. To make assembly easier, you can clamp temporary blocks to the posts to support a triangular floor section as you fasten it, as shown in **F**.

3. Mount the first two pie sections opposite each other, with a connecting block straddling them at the center of the floor, as shown in **G** and the bottom drawing on p. 154.

4. Install the remaining floor sections and connecting blocks, as shown in **H** (on p. 158). When all the connecting blocks are in place there will be even gaps between neighboring floor sections because the blocks are the same thickness as the posts. Note that there is one

WHAT CAN GO WRONG

If any of the 2×4 posts are crooked, plane them straight before setting them in position. Otherwise you may have trouble slipping the box posts over them.

PRO TIP

Before running in all the screws, check to make sure the floor section is level. If not, raise or lower the appropriate corner in relation to the post.

5. Nail together the cedar box posts that will cover the 2×4 posts, but leave off the inside face for now, as shown in **I**. The resulting U-shaped box post can then slip easily over the 2×4. Two opposing sides of the box post extend above the top of the 2×4 like a pair of ears with pointed tops. Eventually, these ears will capture the sides of the hip rafters that sit atop the posts. The third side of the box post, which is shorter than the other two sides, is cut square across. The 2×4 posts will eventually be trimmed flush with the tops of these lower square-cut sides.

6. Install the outermost course of floorboards around the perimeter of the floor, as shown in **J**. A rough fit between the floorboards and the 2×4 posts is acceptable here, because the box posts will cover any gaps.

Vertical skirt boards will eventually wrap around the perimeter of the gazebo floor, hiding the rough lumber used to construct the pie sections. It's best to wait a month after framing

long block (the first to be installed) and four shorter ones that butt into it. In addition to acting as a spacer, the long block forms a strong tie between opposing pie sections. Some of the four short blocks are single bevel and some are double bevel. The bevels are cut at 60 degrees, like most of the cuts for this project. Refer to your full-scale drawing when cutting these pieces.

Roof Mock-Up for Accuracy

BEFORE INSTALLING THE LAST FLOOR SECTION, you can use it as a base to build a partial mock-up of the roof frame. Making a mock-up allows you to test the accuracy of your roof framing cuts on the ground, which is easier and safer than doing it 8 ft. above the ground. When used as a mock-up, one edge of the simulated roof frame represents the 2×6 header that will eventually support the jack rafters. A block nailed to the side of the floor frame simulates the top of a post where a hip rafter will bear. To hold the hexagonal centerpost up in the air you will need to attach it to a sort of hat stand that can be crudely constructed of whatever lumber you have on hand. Use a spirit level or a plumb bob to make sure the centerline of the post is propped up directly above the simulated centerpoint of the gazebo.

Take the time to get your roof frame accurate before you finish the floor—and while you're still on the ground.

the gazebo to install the skirt boards, however, because shrinkage in the underlying framing can cause gaps to open where the skirt boards meet at the corners. If that happens (as it did when I built this project), the gaps can be covered with corner blocks.

Frame

To finish the "walls" of the gazebo, you'll need to install the box posts and the headers, as well as the trim boards.

1. Using one of the box posts as a gauge, mark the tops of all the rough 2×4 posts, as shown in **A**. (Be sure to scribe along the low, square side of the box post, not along the extended "ears.") Then cut the tops of the rough 2×4 posts square with a jigsaw, leaving them all the same height, as shown in **B** on p. 160. Slip the box posts over the 2×4 posts and fasten them

A

SAFETY FIRST

When firing an air nailer with one hand, keep your other hand at least several inches away. Air nails can be driven off course by knots in a board.

3. After bracing the posts, check the distance between the tops of opposite posts, as shown in **D**. It should match the full-scale half-plan you drew on the plywood (see Step 1 on p. 154). This dimension should also check out with your rafter layout when you get to the roof-framing stage. Before raising the rafters you can lay them on the ground to check their span.

4. Cut the headers with 60-degree bevels on both ends, taking their length from the plan. Install the headers between the tops of the box posts using screws, as shown in **E**. When all the headers are installed the posts should be parallel to each other, but they'll still be wobbly and perhaps slightly out of plumb from side to side. You will correct that soon.

5. Use finish nails to install the soffits and frieze boards (the trim boards that finish off the headers), as shown in **F**. Then install the decorative brackets at the corners of each opening. Be sure to check that the posts are plumb as you're installing the brackets, as shown in **G**. The brackets aren't just for looks; they help to stiffen the posts from side to side and hold them plumb.

with finish nails. The inside faces of the box posts can be added now, or you can wait until after the roof is constructed.

2. Use 2×4s to brace the posts in a plumb position from inside to outside. (The posts may still sway from side to side for the time being.) The bottoms of the braces can slide between the floor triangles and be temporarily secured with screws. The pointed tops of the 2×4 braces are screwed to the posts, as shown in **C**.

Roof

The gazebo is taking shape, and you're ready to begin the roof framing. After all the rafters are installed you may want to tie them together with a steel cable to prevent them from spreading apart at the base of the roof (see the sidebar on p. 163).

1. To build a working platform, lay a temporary 2×10 plank across the top of the gazebo, securing it with screws. Then cut shorter planks to reach to the other four sides of the gazebo, screwing them down as well, as shown in **H**. Check your plan to locate the planks so they won't conflict with the jack rafters that are to come. Where the planks meet in the middle, fasten a temporary 4×4 post underneath for support.

2. The hip rafters will all converge at a hexagonal centerpost. The post can be ripped on a tablesaw, setting the blade tilt at 30 degrees. If you're handy with a lathe (or you know a cabinetmaker who is) you can further embellish the center post with a turned finial. Lay the center post on the ground, then screw the first pair

of hip rafters to it, as shown in **I** (on p. 162). Hoist the resulting V-shaped assembly into position. An extra helper or two is helpful at this point. After setting the hip rafters in place, secure them by screwing through the ears that project from the tops of the box posts, as shown in **J** (on p. 162).

I

J

K

PRO**TIP**

Sheathing boards diminish in length on a given side, going from longest at the bottom to shortest at the top. If you mock up a one-sixth section of the roof on the ground, you can precut your boards for all six sides at the same time. They should all be the same length in each course.

SCAFFOLD PLANK ARRANGEMENT

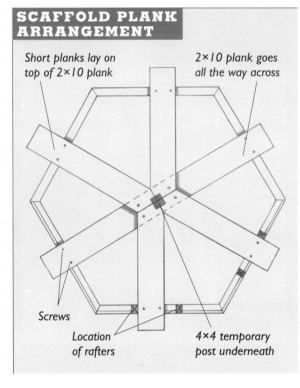

Short planks lay on top of 2×10 plank

2×10 plank goes all the way across

Screws

Location of rafters

4×4 temporary post underneath

L

3. Set another pair of opposing hip rafters in place, fastening them at the bottom only. Check where the tops of these rafters bear against the center post. If the tops of the newly set rafters don't line up, rock the first pair of rafters left or right. This will cause the tops of the rafters to slide against the center post until the problem is corrected. Then screw the tops of the rafters to the center post, as shown in **K**. Install the final pair of rafters the same way.

4. Screw the purlins in place on the hip rafters, as shown in **L**, and then screw in the jack rafters. Make sure that the lower ends of the jack rafters line up with the ends of the hip rafters, so the trim will go on nicely. If any of the jack rafters need trimming, you can nip them with a jigsaw.

5. Sheathe the roof. This gazebo employs spaced skip sheathing, which allows the overlying cedar shingles to dry out quickly. For an asphalt shingle roof you would use plywood or solid boards instead of skip sheathing.

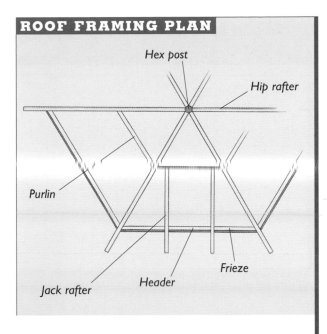

ROOF FRAMING PLAN

Hex post

Hip rafter

Purlin

Jack rafter

Header

Frieze

Reinforcing the Ceiling

ALL PITCHED ROOFS HAVE A TENDENCY TO SAG over time unless their opposite sides are tied together somehow. As the weight of the roof pushes down, the base of the roof wants to spread apart, which in turn allows the ridge or apex to fall. A flat ceiling will counteract this force by tying the base of the roof together, but what if you don't want a flat ceiling? In that case, you can encircle the gazebo with a steel tension cable hidden in the cornice to keep the base of the roof from spreading.

Drill holes in each of the hip rafters. The holes should be slightly larger in diameter than the cable—there's no need for a tight fit. Drill holes in the jack rafters as well so the cable can pass from hip to hip in a straight line. Then thread the cable through all the holes and join the two ends with a turnbuckle. Tighten the turnbuckle until the cable feels taut.

A woven steel cable is hidden within the cornice. It extends around the entire roof to keep the bottoms of the rafters from spreading apart.

Skip Sheathing vs. Solid Sheathing

SKIP SHEATHING IS A METHOD OF COVERING a roof frame with spaced boards or strips rather than tightly fitted boards. This configuration improves air circulation under the roof covering, which helps prevent rot in both the roof covering and the roof frame. The roof covering laid over a skip-sheathed roof must be stiff enough to bridge across the gaps between the sheathing boards. Wood shingles, slate shingles, and metal standing-seam roofing meet this requirement. Asphalt shingles are more flexible, however, so they require solid sheathing for support.

When shingles are laid over skip sheathing, the spacing of the shingle courses equals the spacing of the sheathing strips or boards. On a flat roof this spacing can be easily laid out with a tape measure. However, on a concave roof, such as the one featured here, the spacing of the skip sheathing must be laid out along a curve. Using a compass, set the distance between the compass points to equal the shingle spacing, and then "walk" the compass along the curve, marking as you go.

Pressure-treated 1×2 skip sheathing provides a nail base for the shingles, which allows the underside of the shingles to dry out. (Shingling is halfway completed, as seen from the interior).

Finishing up

At this point, you need to finish up the trim, the floor, and the roof and install any details, like a railing.

1. Install the bed molding, fascia, and crown molding, in that order, as shown in **A**. All of the ends are cut at a 60-degree angle.

2. Backfill the post holes with concrete, stopping 3 in. below grade, as shown in **B**. (Fill the remaining 3 in. with dirt later so grass can grow.) Allow the concrete to harden for a day, and then remove the temporary post braces.

3. Finish installing the concentric floorboards. At the center use a hexagonal piece cut from a wide board, as shown in **C**, which will look better than six little pie-shaped pieces crammed together.

4. Shingle the roof, as shown in **D**. This gazebo was roofed with cedar shingles, but a heavy "architectural" asphalt shingle would make a satisfactory substitute. Roofing techniques are beyond the scope of this book; if you need help with roofing techniques, try *Roofing with Asphalt Shingles* by Mike Guertin (The Taunton Press, 2002) or *For Pros by Pros: Roofing, Flashing, & Waterproofing* (The Taunton Press, 2005).

5. Install the railing. A complicated railing such as the one built for this gazebo is best prefabricated flat on a workbench, using a full-scale plywood template as a guide. Use stainless-steel trim screws to join the various angled members together. For a simple railing composed of vertical spindles you don't need a template, and you can use galvanized or stainless-steel finish nails instead of screws.

First cut the top and bottom rails to length. Lay out the locations of the spindles on one of the top rails first, and then transfer the layout to the other top rails and all the bottom rails. Nail the railings together on a flat surface (such as a patio). First drive long finish nails through the top and bottom rails into the ends of the spindles, and then toenail small finish nails diagonally through the spindles into the rails. The through-nails alone might pull out because they go into the spindle's end grain, but the toenails (which penetrate across the grain of both pieces) will keep the joints tight. Install the railings as units, toenailing the top and bottom rails to the posts.

SAFETY FIRST

To access the roof for shingling, you need a scaffold. It can be a set of tall, well-braced sawhorses, or manufactured steel pipe scaffolding. Pipe scaffolding can be furnished with special manufactured walkboards for maximum safety. When using wooden planks as walkboards, make sure they are rated for scaffold use and don't position their underlying supports more than 8 ft. apart. Don't ever build a scaffold with stepladders because they aren't wide enough to be stable, especially on uneven ground.

DESIGN
OPTIONS

▸ The hefty earth-toned
posts of this gazebo
mimic nearby trees,
helping the structure
to rest comfortably in
the landscape.

◀ An elegant gazebo is mysteriously reflected in a nearby pond, causing the already-shimmering appearance of the scrollsawn balustrade to be amplified even further.

▲ This gazebo's open-slat roof and croquet-ball finial give it a sunny disposition.

◀ The rugged good looks of this timber-framed gazebo come from natural materials arranged with careful proportions and strict classical symmetry.

APPENDIX 1: Planning Outdoor Structures

Finding Inspiration

The first thing to do is to visualize specific solutions for your site. Scour the library shelves for gardening books and magazines, and check out nurseries and home centers for brochures and project books with simple patterns.

Gardens that have been carefully thought out, such as parks, arboretums, and historic restorations, can also provide inspiration. Bring a camera along to take pictures of what you like. You might also use a tape measure and a sketch book to record the dimensions of features you particularly admire.

If you see a handsome project in your neighborhood, swallow your embarrassment and go knock on the front door. Gardeners are as vain about their accomplishments as anyone, and most will be delighted to give a tour to a friendly admirer. Ask them where they obtained their materials. If a contractor did the work, get his name and number so that you can ask him questions.

Once you have some ideas, you can begin planning your project in earnest. This involves checking out what materials are available in your area, making a photo mockup, and heading to the drawing board to make a set of plans.

Available materials

A visit to the local building supply is a good idea before sitting down at the drawing board. Wander around the place to get an idea of what's available and try to get a sense of which items are affordable and which ones will break the bank.

In the showroom you'll see all kinds of problem-solving fasteners and hardware. Premanufactured specialty items such as lattice panels and finials can enhance a design while simplifying its execution. Tell a salesperson about your project and ask them to steer you toward appropriate materials.

A paper mockup can be taped or pasted onto a photo to help visualize an arbor-to-be.

In the lumberyard you can check out wood in all shapes, sizes, textures, and species. If a burly fellow comes up and asks to see your sales ticket, tell him you're just browsing. This may illicit a confused or disapproving look on his face, but ignore it—you have the right to look around.

Photo mockups

The most effective way to visualize what your landscape project will look like is to prepare a photo mockup. Begin by shooting a roll of film at the proposed building site, taking shots from different angles. A wide-angle lens is ideal for this, but a regular 50mm lens works fine. Put a person or a piece of furniture in the picture several feet from where the project will be to help you to get a handle on the scale of the project when you start to draw in the structure.

Have a set of large prints made (at least 4×6). Place a sheet of tracing paper over one of the photos and sketch in your idea. You don't need to include a lot of detail or have the right perspective; what you're mainly concerned with here is scale. Try several different sizes, even if they seem too big or too small. When you get a sense of the

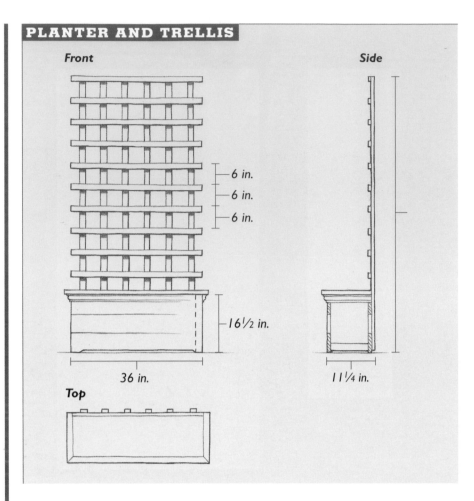

PLANTER AND TRELLIS

Front

6 in.
6 in.
6 in.

16½ in.

36 in.

Top

Side

11¼ in.

appropriate size, make a paper cutout and color it with colored pencils. Place the cutout on the photo and slide it around until you zero in on just the right spot (see the photo on p. 169). Do the same with the photos taken from different angles.

With a digital camera and some computer savvy you can generate a digital mock-up. Software such as Photoshop is terrific for this because you can instantly manipulate characteristics such as size and color.

Working drawings

Creating a set of working drawings does more than just give you a road map to follow when the chips start flying. It actually forces you to think through problems of proportion, joinery, and sequencing ahead of time. This planning gives

you the opportunity to head off problems before they arise, perhaps by deciding to shift a crosspiece to a different location or by using a larger post.

Thinking in two dimensions is a talent given more to some than to others. But regardless of your level of skill with a pencil, it's worth a try. Remember, you're not trying to paint a masterpiece; you're just rehearsing the building process in a very cost-effective way. (Paper is cheap; lumber is not.) Begin with freehand sketches on cheap copy paper. Surround yourself with the photos you've found and the photo mockups you've made. Don't be afraid to experiment with different sizes, shapes, and details. When you've settled on a design, it's time to render working drawings to scale (see the drawing above).

To start with, you will need to settle on a scale for your drawing. For most of the projects in this book, a scale of ½ in. = 1 ft. works well. This scale is large enough to allow you to include details but small enough to fit your drawing on a standard 8½×11 sheet of paper. For a large project, such as a retaining wall, you would use a smaller scale, such as ¼ in. = 1 ft. or even ⅛ in. = 1 ft. For close-up details like brackets or corner intersections, you would use a larger scale, such as 1 in. = 1 ft., or simply draw them full scale (actual size).

To render measurements in the appropriate scale, an architect's rule comes in handy. It's a three-edged ruler, with different scales laid out on each edge. If you don't have an architect's rule, just use a plain ruler. If you're working in ½-in. scale, each inch will represent 2 ft. So,

if you were drawing a 6-ft. post, for instance, it would measure 3 in. on your drawing. Measurements of less than a foot can be estimated, knowing that each ⅛-in. increment on the plain ruler represents one quarter of a whole foot, or 3 in.

A simple, effective way to produce scale drawings without drafting tools is to use graph paper. For small projects, I like the kind that has heavy 1-in. squares subdivided into lighter ¼-in. squares. At a scale of 1 in. = 1 ft., the heavy squares represent feet and the lighter squares represent 3-in. increments. This arrangement makes it easy to reference a feet/inches measurement on the drawing. At this scale, a standard 8½×11 sheet of paper will accommodate projects up to 8 ft. by 10 ft.—perfect for an arbor or trellis.

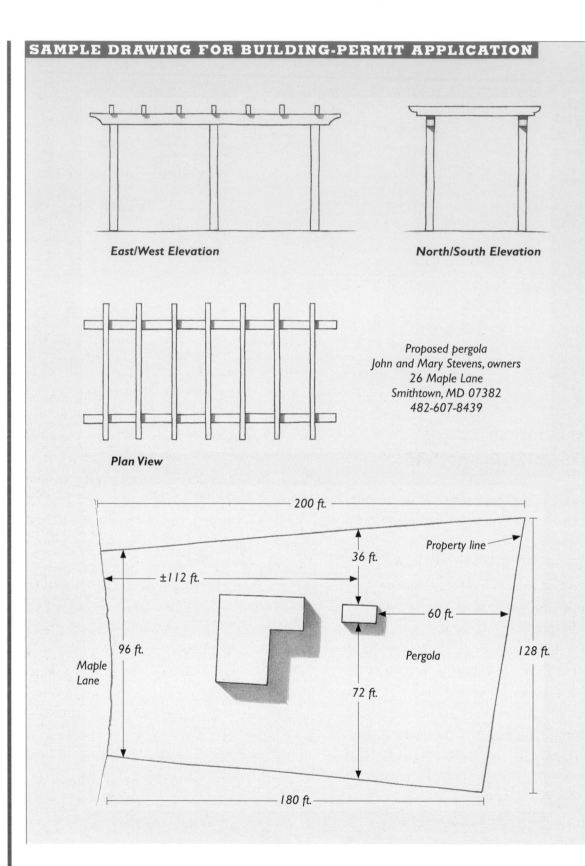

SAMPLE DRAWING FOR BUILDING-PERMIT APPLICATION

East/West Elevation

North/South Elevation

Plan View

Proposed pergola
John and Mary Stevens, owners
26 Maple Lane
Smithtown, MD 07382
482-607-8439

200 ft.

Property line

36 ft.

±112 ft.

60 ft.

96 ft.

128 ft.

Maple
Lane

Pergola

72 ft.

180 ft.

Variances

Obtaining Building Permits and Variances

Before undertaking any major outdoor building project, call your local building department (it will be listed in the local government section of your phone directory). Describe your project to one of the building officials, giving some idea of its size. The official may also ask for the approximate distance from the proposed project to your property line. If the project is small enough, the official may wave you ahead with no further ado. In other cases, you will be asked to apply for a permit. Localities vary widely in the stringency of their requirements, so don't assume anything.

A building permit serves several functions. First, it ensures that your project will be built according to certain minimum quality standards. For instance, your local code might require the use of pressure-treated lumber for outdoor projects. Second, a permit ensures that the structure conforms to local zoning ordinances. For instance, fences in residential zones are usually limited to a height of 6 ft. Third, if you have an architectural review board (ARB) in your local ity, the permit will require that your design be reviewed. The ARB will determine whether your design is compatible with the prevailing architectural climate of the community. In some cases, the ARB will make suggestions, such as adding finials to a gate post or specifying the color of a fence. Finally, a building permit is used to adjust real estate assessments for local tax rolls. For this reason, you will be asked to show the estimated cost of construction for your project.

Although you can apply for a permit through the mail, it's quicker to visit the building department. Bring along a simple sketch of the project and a photocopy of the plot plan of your property, also called a plat. (A plat is usually attached to your property deed.) Indicate the project's location on the photocopy. Sometimes, though, you can simply draw a thumbnail sketch of your property and show rough dimensions on it (for an example, see the facing page). For most garden projects, these simple drawings will be all that's required to file a permit application. If the officials want more detailed drawings, they'll let you know.

A building permit issued for a major structure, such as a home, will require inspections at different stages in the building process. Inspections are not usually required for the kinds of projects described in this book, but if they are, the necessary inspections will be described on the permit. For instance, if you were building a pergola, the building department might want to inspect the depth of your post holes to make sure they are deep enough. In that case, you would need to call the building department after you had dug the holes to have them inspected by a building official. Once the official OKed the holes, you could proceed with the work.

Sometimes, the project you've chosen to build may violate a local building code. For instance, suppose you want to build an arbor 6 ft. from your property line, but the code in your town requires 15 ft. minimum of clearance between such a structure and any boundary. In such a case, you'd need a variance, which is a special permit that allows you to build something that would not normally be permissible under existing ordinances. You may be required to show hardship to have this kind of exception made. You will also need the consent of your neighbors.

Estimating and Ordering Materials

Having finished a complete set of working drawings, you should have a good idea of the materials you'll need. Before preparing a formal bill of materials (a builder's shopping list), simply list the various components of the structure on a separate sheet of paper. Don't worry about how many or how much at this point. You're simply making a checklist here so that you don't overlook anything.

After completing the checklist, you can begin the actual bill of materials (a sample bill is shown on the facing page). Keep it neat. On a sheet of lined paper, draw vertical lines to produce six columns. Start with a "Quantity" column, which tells how many of a particular item are needed and in what units. For lumber, that would mean the number of pieces for each length. For nails, it would be the number of boxes and the weight per box. (In some places, nails are sold in bulk, so you would simply list pounds of each size.) Many items are sold individually, such as bolts and framing connectors.

Next is the "Item" column. In this column describe the component, with as many particulars as possible. Lumber should be specified as to species and grade. Nails should be listed according to size and type. Give the diameter and length of screws and bolts. (There's more on these particulars in Chapter 1.)

The next column—"Function"—is for your own benefit (not the salesperson's). List the use of each component—for instance, "legs"—so that you'll be able to untangle the order when it's delivered. If you plan on cutting pieces into shorter lengths or narrower widths, note that here as well.

The last three columns are where the arithmetic occurs. The "Extension" column is a distillation of the "Quantity" column. The extension is the number actually used to multiply the unit price (price per foot, pound, or whatever) to arrive at the total cost for that item. For instance, say you need two different lengths of post, eight footers and six footers. The quantity/item would be listed as "two 8 ft." and "four 6 ft.," respectively. If your supplier sells 4×4 lumber by the foot, the extension would be lumped together at 40 ([2 × 8] + [4 × 6] = 40); if the supplier sells

Sample Bill of Materials for Rose Arbor

Quantity	Item	Function	Extension	Unit price	Cost
8	1×4×8 ft. PT	Legs—outer layers			
3	1×4×8 ft. PT	Cross slats—rip to 1¾ in.	11	$1.36 ea.	$14.96
1	1×4×10 ft. PT	Legs—inner blocking	1	$1.63 ea.	$1.63
4	80-lb. concrete mix		4	$3.99 ea.	$15.95
5 lb.	6d galvanized finish nail		5	$0.86/lb.	$4.30
1 lb.	1⅝-in. galvanized screw		1	$3.50/lb.	$3.50
4	1×8×8 clear cedar	Segment pieces			
1	1×8×8 clear cedar	Dogleg pieces	40	$2.75/ft.	$110.00
				Subtotal	
				Tax	
				Total	

lumber by the piece, two extensions would be used (2 and 4, respectively). In another example, you might list several different sizes of bulk nails under the "Quantity"/"Item" columns and then combine them into total pounds under the "Extension" column.

Confusion may arise when you present your bill of materials at the lumberyard, owing to the wide variety of pricing practices in the building materials trade. For instance, some types of lumber are priced the same per foot in all different lengths, whereas other types are sold with a premium on long lengths. In the latter case, lumber is sold by the piece rather than by the total footage. As long as your list is carefully itemized, the salesperson can work this out with you.

Once you have your bill of materials drawn up, you can put it out for bid. Fax or e-mail an unpriced copy of the list to several different suppliers in your area to find the best price. Bear in mind, however, that the lowest price isn't always the best value. Verify things like delivery charges and return policies. A visit to a supplier is the best way to get a sense of the service you can expect.

APPENDIX 2: Choosing Wood

The wood species you choose for your project will greatly affect its durability and appearance.

Softwoods and hardwoods In botany, the term "softwood" applies to needle-bearing trees, whereas "hardwood" refers to broad-leaved trees. Most softwood trees are also coniferous (cone-bearing) and evergreen (the exceptions to the latter being cypress and larch, which shed their needles in the fall).

In carpentry, the terms hardwood and softwood refer to the wood itself. Hardwoods, such as oak, cherry, and maple, come from hardwood trees, whereas softwoods, such as pine, cedar, and redwood, come from softwood trees. In general, wood from the softwood family of trees is softer, and thus easier to work, than hardwood lumber, but there are exceptions. Poplar is a broad-leaved

This redwood board contains both heartwood, which is red, and sapwood, which is cream colored. Heartwood is much more decay resistant than sapwood.

hardwood tree whose wood is almost as soft as pine, whereas larch is a softwood that is quite hard.

Naturally decay-resistant woods Long before man-made preservatives arrived on the scene, woodworkers observed that certain woods lasted longer outside than others. These woods, which include redwood, cedar, cypress, locust, oak, and a few tropical hardwoods, contain natural oils that inhibit decay. Most decay-inhibiting oils are found in heartwood, which is the older, nonliving part of a tree. Sapwood is the outer wood, where sap flow occurs through living cells. Boards may contain varying amounts of heartwood and sapwood, depending on how they are cut from a log. The heartwood, which tends to be dark in color, will usually be found at the center of a board, whereas the light-colored sapwood is found at the edges (see the photo at left). When ordering certain species of lumber, you may be able to specify "all heart." You can also trim off the sapwood yourself for maximum decay resistance.

Redwood comes from two species: the coast redwood, which grows along the California coast, and the sequoia, which grows farther inland. Redwood is light, stable, and highly decay resistant. Clear, all-heart redwood that's been

Woods for Landscape Carpentry

Species or Type	Pros	Cons	Expense	Best Application
Redwood	• Excellent workability • Excellent decay resistance • Widespread availability, especially on West Coast	• Low strength	• Low for construction grade • Moderate for clear grade that includes sapwood • High for clear all-heart (CAH) grade	• Construction grade: raised beds (including edibles), borders, rough fences • Finish grades: arbors, trellises, pergolas, fancy fences, gazebo finish materials
Western red cedar	• Good to excellent workability • Excellent decay resistance in all-heart grades; moderate in grades that include sapwood • Widespread availability	• Low strength	• Moderate for construction grades • High for premium grades	• See Redwood
Eastern white cedar	• Easy to cut • Very good decay resistance • Widely available as manufactured items such as fence posts	• Coarse texture • Low strength • Raw lumber is difficult to find/buy	• Moderate	• See Redwood
Cypress	• Excellent workability • Excellent decay resistance in heartwood; moderate in sapwood	• Tends to check and peel in bright sunlight • Low strength • Hard to find outside southeastern U.S.	• Moderate	• See Redwood
PT yellow pine, PT Douglas fir	• Good workability with power tools • Excellent decay resistance • Good strength • Widespread availability for yellow pine	• Difficult to work with hand tools • Sensitive to UV degradation • Douglas fir available only in western states • Douglas fir must be perforated, which makes it unsightly	• Low	• Construction grades: retaining walls, raised beds (ornamentals), rough fences, borders • Premium grades: arbors, trellises, pergolas, gates, fancy fences, decking, gazebo framing lumber
Locust	• Excellent decay resistance • Excellent strength	• Difficult to work • Available only in local sawmills in eastern U.S.	• Low	• Fence posts, woodland steps, and borders
White oak	• Good decay resistance • Excellent strength • Widespread availability as a cabinet wood; sold "green" at local sawmills in Midwest and eastern U.S. at low cost	• Difficult to work	• Moderate to high as kiln-dried sold at lumberyards • Low as green wood sold at sawmills	• Above-grade applications such as gates, fences, and decking
Ipé, greenheart, purpleheart	• Excellent decay resistance • Excellent strength • Ipé widely available	• Very heavy • Greenheart and purpleheart may be hard to find • Moderate to high	• Moderate to high	• Arbors, pergolas, gates, decking, gazebo flooring
Honduras mahogany	• Excellent workability • Good decay resistance • Good strength		• Very high	• See Ipé
Phillipine mahogany (lauan)	• Good workability • Good decay resistance • Good strength		• Moderate to high	• See Ipé
Teak	• Superb decay resistance • Very good strength	• Very difficult to work	• Out of sight	• See Ipé

cut from virgin forests is available, but it's very expensive. For most outdoor projects, a grade known as "con-heart" is a good choice. Con-heart, which is cut primarily from plantation-grown redwood, contains knots but no sapwood. Knots can be difficult to work around because of their hardness, but they don't affect durability. In fact, knots contain even more preservative oils than the surrounding heartwood.

Cedar has a somewhat coarser grain than redwood but still works easily. Several varieties are available in North America, but the two major groups are western and eastern cedar. Western red cedar grows primarily in Washington State and British Columbia. It has an orange to brown color. The eastern, or Atlantic, white cedar comes mostly from eastern Canada. It runs from cream to light orange in color. Western red cedar is the more decay-resistant of the two.

There are a few less-available species of cedar as well. Alaska cedar has a yellow color and a wonderful smell when it's cut. Incense cedar (an aromatic species used to line wardrobe closets) runs pink to purple in color. Because incense cedar trees are small, boards tend to be narrow and knotty. Port Orford cedar is a premium cedar prized for its fine working characteristics.

Cypress grows in the marshy areas of the southeastern United States. When virgin swamps were cut at the beginning of this century, vast quantities of wide heartwood cypress lumber, which has excellent decay resistance, were pro-duced. Today, most of the cypress logs harvested are small in diameter and contain mainly sapwood, which has only moderate decay resistance. Sapwood cypress is a light cream color, whereas heartwood is an orange-gold. A disadvantage of cypress is that its grain tends to peel in bright sunlight. Cypress also checks more than redwood or cedar, but for rustic garden work, these defects are not usually a problem.

Two eastern hardwoods have natural decay resistance—locust and white oak. Both of these woods are dense, hard, and difficult to work with. They're also less stable than the softwoods mentioned here. If you can find these woods at a local sawmill, however, the price can make them attractive.

Locust is a smallish tree with olive-green heartwood. It's often used for fence posts. White oak is available in large timber sizes as well as boards. The acids in white oak—called tannin—give this species its decay resistance. The same acids cause white oak to turn black when exposed to the weather.

The forests of South America, Asia, and Africa produce many tropical hardwoods with excellent decay resistance. They tend to be extremely dense, which makes them challenging to work with. On the other hand, their density can be an advantage for high-wear surfaces such as decking. A few of the better known species are ipé, greenheart, and purpleheart. Honduras mahogany and Philippine mahogany (lauan) are moderately dense tropical woods that are workable and highly stable. As a result, they're used a lot in boat building. And mahogany is more readily available than the other tropicals. As a fine cabinet wood, though, mahogany's price is steep. Teak is another fine cabinet wood. It is one of the most decay-resistant species in the world, but it is very expensive and rather difficult to work.

SAFETY FIRST

When working with lumber or railroad ties that have been treated with either penta or creosote, observe even stricter precautions than you would when using CCA-treated lumber. Always wear heavy clothing and gloves, and use a rubber respirator instead of a dust mask for maximum lung protection.

The Safety of Pressure-Treated Wood

THE GROWING USE OF PRESSURE-TREATED LUMBER has raised concerns about safety. CCA, the copper compound formerly used for pressure treatment, was banned for residential use in 2004. The compounds that have replaced CCA are considered safer. The wood-treatment industry offers assurances about the safety of their products, but they also urge that certain precautions be taken when working with pressure-treated lumber. Don't cut or sand the stuff inside, and wear goggles and a dust mask. Gloves are also a good idea, especially when handling wet lumber right off the pile. Sometimes a liquid residue of the treatment chemical is present that hasn't been fully absorbed into the wood. If a dry residue of chemical is apparent on the surface, then don't use that board where it will contact persons, such as for a seat. Wash your hands after working with pressure-treated lumber, and wash your clothes separately from the rest of your household laundry.

One very real danger of pressure-treated wood is the formation of toxic gases and ashes by combustion. Never burn pressure-treated scraps or sawdust in stoves, fireplaces, or even the open air. Instead, dispose of the waste at a landfill or by regular trash collection. Use a plastic groundcover to catch the sawdust generated by your saw.

The safety of pressure-treated lumber has been questioned for more than 25 years.

Manufacturers advise against the use of pressure-treated lumber in the following circumstances:

- Where the preservative may become a component of food or animal feed.
- For beehives.
- In direct or indirect contact with drinking water.

Pressure-treated wood Wood can also be treated with chemicals to make it resistant to decay and insects. The chemicals can be applied in either of two ways: surface treatment or pressure treatment. Surface treatment—the less effective method—is discussed in the section on finishes (see p. 23). Pressure treatment involves forcing chemicals into wood under high pressure. Ideally, the chemicals are distributed throughout the wood's entire cell structure, not just near the surface; this makes pressure treatment the most effective method of wood preserving. It's the only method recommended for wood that will be placed in contact with the ground or below grade.

Three different classes of chemicals are used in pressure treatment. The first two, creosote and pentachlorophenol (penta), are not generally recommended for residential use. At one time they were available in liquid form for field application, but they are now classified as restricted-use pesticides. Wood treated with these chemicals is still available in the form of railroad ties. The third class of chemicals used for pressure treatment is a family of copper-based compounds. Lumber treated with these compounds is safer and easier to use than lumber treated with either creosote or penta, and has become the standard for residential use. However one of these copper-based compounds, CCA, was banned for residential applications as of January 1, 2004, because of concerns about safety and environmental health (see the sidebar above). Taking the place of CCA are two other copper compounds, ACQ and CA.

When you ask for pressure-treated wood at the local lumberyard it will be treated with one of these two chemicals.

Both ACQ and CA have a proven track record, so you can use either with confidence. What's most important, however, is that you specify either "ground contact" or "above ground" as the intended use. For example, a post buried in the ground needs the higher amount of chemical indicated by a "ground contact" rating, whereas a gate rail can get by with the lower amount of chemical indicated by an "above ground" rating.

Certain woods accept pressure treatment better than others. In the eastern United States, almost all pressure-treated lumber is southern yellow pine. In the west, Douglas fir is pressure treated as well, although it doesn't take preservative as well as pine due to its cellular structure. To compensate for this, fir must be perforated—a process that makes the wood unsightly.

Yellow pine and fir have a hard, stringy texture that makes them difficult to work with hand tools. Although pressure-treated wood is paintable, the stringiness of the species used prevents the material from holding a finish as well as some of the finer-grained softwoods mentioned earlier. The high moisture content of most PT lumber also affects paintability and workability. Unless it's been kiln dried after treatment, PT lumber should be seasoned on site (see p. 18). PT lumber that has been dried after treatment will bear the letters "KDAT" on the grade stamp or label.

Composites As forest-products technology has advanced, man-made materials for outdoor use have appeared. Some of them, such as plywood, come in sizes that are not readily available in solid lumber. Others, such as wood-polymer lumber and all-plastic lumber, offer superior durability in an outdoors environment.

Plywood—one of the first man-made wood products—consists of multiple wood veneers laminated together to form a sheet. Its great advantage lies in its ability to cover large areas quickly. Plywood's weakness lies in its laminated edge, which is unsightly and doesn't hold fasteners well. Plywood also has trouble staying flat on its own, especially when wet. It will sag and warp unless supported by a framework of some kind. For these reasons, plywood is best used either as a skin to cover a frame (such as the siding of a garden shed) or as a panel that fits inside a frame (such as a flat-panel gate).

Plywoods for outdoor use can be divided into two categories: PT construction-grade plywood and marine plywood. PT construction-grade

Ground Contact vs. Above Ground

WOOD THAT'S RATED FOR GROUND CONTACT retains more chemical after treatment than wood that's rated for above-ground use (about 0.4 lb./cu. ft. for ground contact versus .125 lb./cu. ft. for above ground). Even higher retention levels can be special ordered for extreme-duty applications such as docks and wood foundations.

In general, posts and poles are treated for ground contact only, but boards are treated for both ground-contact and above-ground use. (There's a third category, "decking," as well.) Be sure to specify what you need when you buy. To make sure you're getting the retention level you paid for you can inspect the little tag that's stapled to the end of the board. It will state the end-use application in the upper right corner (see the example below). Some manufacturers color-code their tags to make the difference more obvious.

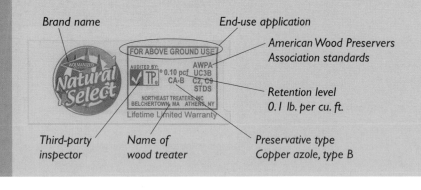

Brand name

End-use application

American Wood Preservers Association standards

Retention level
0.1 lb. per cu. ft.

Third-party inspector

Name of wood treater

Preservative type
Copper azole, type B

plywood is a rough product suitable for ground-contact applications such as foundations. It's available in the same species as PT woods. Sheet thicknesses of ½ in. and ¾ in. are readily available in the standard 4×8 size.

Marine plywood is a very high grade of exterior plywood made specifically for boat building. It is not pressure treated, but most of the species used, such as mahogany and teak, have natural decay resistance. It is also assumed that a finish will be applied and regularly maintained to provide protection from the elements. Marine plywood can be used in the garden for above-grade applications. Its high cost ($100 per sheet and up) may be justified for high-end projects, where premium species of solid lumber are used as well. Marine plywood is sold in a much wider variety of sizes than PT plywood. Thickness ranges from ⅛ in. through 1 in., and sheet sizes of 4×10, 4×12, and 4×16 are available in addition to the standard 4×8.

As the supply of large, old-growth trees has dwindled, manufacturers have looked for ways to make heavy beams from smaller logs. The result is engineered lumber, an umbrella term for various types of man-made wooden beams.

One type of engineered lumber is the "glulam" beam (short for glue-laminated). It's essentially a stack of small boards glued face to face to make one large beam. In spite of its composite makeup, glulams may be as strong as naturally grown timber of the same size. In fact, glulams often carry a higher strength rating than natural timbers of the same size because the boards used inside a glulam are inspected before manufacturing. The inspection prevents a glulam from having the kinds of severe knots or splits that are sometimes hidden inside natural timbers.

Glulams for exposed outdoor use are laminated with waterproof glue and pressure treated

The wide, unbroken span of this pergola is carried by main beams of parallel-strand lumber. The lighter boards between the main beams are solid wood.

against decay. Curved glulams can be custom laminated on special curved forms. The combination of graceful shapes with high strength makes curved glulams good for garden bridges as well as large pergolas.

A newer type of engineered lumber is parallel-strand lumber (PSL). PSL is composed of long, thin strands of wood bonded together under high pressure. PSL actually accepts pressure treatment better than solid lumber because it is more porous. You can see this if you compare the cut ends of a regular PT yellow pine 4×4 and a treated PSL 4×4. In the regular 4×4, the green color gives way to yellow toward the center, indicating that CCA retention diminishes away from the surface. The PSL 4×4 shows uniform retention throughout. The sole manufacturer of PSL at present is Trus Joist MacMillan, which sells both a treated and a nontreated product under the brand name Parallam.

When specifying the size of any engineered lumber beam, remember that these products do not necessarily have as much strength as a solid wood beam of the same dimensions. Also, their

Wood-polymer lumber creates a durable, defect-free deck surface.

strength varies, depending on whether they're used above grade or below. When in doubt, consult the manufacturer, an architect, or an engineer.

Another important advance for outdoor woodworking has been the development of wood-polymer lumber. These synthetic products are made from recycled wood and plastic. The result is a material with most of the strength of wood and most (if not all) of the decay resistance of plastic. Lumber made entirely of plastic has also appeared recently. Comparing all of these new products can be bewildering, but an Internet search or a visit to your lumberyard will help you to sort them out.

Wood-polymer and all-plastic lumber can be cut and drilled with ordinary woodworking tools. It has no grain, so there's less splitting when a board is nailed close to its end. On the downside, the lack of grain makes for a rather drab, industrial appearance that may not fit in with natural surroundings.

At present, wood-polymer and all-plastic lumber is produced primarily as boards to be used for decking and seating (see the photo at left). Because they deflect, or bend, more than natural lumber, these products are not currently recommended for structural framing members such as posts and beams. In terms of price, composite decking runs 10 percent to 40 percent higher than premium cedar, and 140 percent (almost three times as much) as premium PT yellow pine.

Timbers for landscaping There are many types of naturally grown landscaping timbers suitable for the outdoors. Most lumberyards carry PT timbers in sizes like 4×4 and 6×6. Standard lengths range from 8 ft. to 16 ft. in 2-ft. increments, but lengths up to 26 ft. may be available by special order. Yards specializing in treated lumber sometimes stock 4×6s and 8×8s as well. Most PT timbers are planed at the mill, but sometimes they're available roughsawn. The roughsawn texture hides defects, such as knots and checks, and is really more appropriate for garden structures because of its rustic appearance. Another advantage of roughsawn timbers is that they run thicker than planed timbers of the same nominal size. For instance, a planed 6×6 will measure 5½ in. by 5½ in. after planing, whereas a rough 6×6 will actually measure about 6 in. by 6 in. The same is true of smaller lumber sizes, such as 2×4s. However, the smaller sizes are almost always planed before sale, except at sawmills.

PT poles are cheaper than square timbers of the same approximate size. Their round, somewhat irregular shape gives them an organic feel that is appropriate in the garden. But their roundness also makes them more difficult to join together than square timbers. As a compromise, you can get semiround landscape timbers that

An edging of natural logs adds character to this vegetable plot.

are round on two opposing sides and flat on the other two sides. Having a flat top and bottom makes landscape timbers easy to stack and overlap.

Railroad ties that have been salvaged from railroad repair work are an inexpensive alternative to PT timbers. Standard railroad ties measure 7 in. by 9 in. by 8½ ft., and the cost of one of these is less than half the cost of an 8-ft. PT 6×6, which is 6 in. shorter and only measures 5½ in. square. Railroad ties are more difficult to work with than PT timbers, though, for several reasons. For one thing, they're usually cut from hardwoods such as oak rather than the softwoods used for PT timbers. That makes ties heavier and harder to cut and drill. Another problem with ties is that they are treated with creosote, which means extra safety precautions. On the upside, ties have a dark, funky appearance that can blend into a landscape better than PT timbers. Ties work particularly well for steps because their 7-in. thickness makes for a comfortable riser height.

The quality of salvaged railroad ties varies widely. Be sure to inspect the product at your lumberyard before purchasing or placing an

order. A tie that is soft and crumbly is at the end of its useful life.

Logs cut from decay-resistant species such as cedar and locust can be used directly in the garden without being squared off (see the photo above). Indeed, the natural appearance of a log is desirable, although its roundness makes joinery a challenge. The bark of a log also adds to its rustic appearance. Unfortunately, bark tends to slough off after just a few seasons, especially when the log is placed directly on the ground. If you want the bark to stay on as long as possible, cut the tree down in winter, when its sap content is at a low point. Conversely, if you intend to peel the bark off the log before using it, fell the tree in summer, when the sap content is high. The sap running between the wood and the bark causes the bark to peel off more easily.

To peel bark, you can buy a specialized tool called a bark spud, which looks like an overgrown chisel. As an alternative, you can hew the bark off with a hatchet or try shoveling it off with a garden spade. Leaving a log outside for a season or two allows nature to do much of the work, as bugs and microbes attack the sugar-laden tissues just below the bark.

INDEX

types of, 92–99
vertical-board, 95–96
finishes, 23–26
avoiding for weathered appearance, 24
decay protection from darker shades of, 14
paints, 25–26
stains, 24–25
sunlight protection from opaque, 15
varnishes, 24
water repellents and preservatives, 23–24
finishing techniques, 42–45
brushing, 43–44
dipping, 43
preparing the surface, 42–43
rolling, 44
spraying, 44–45
frame construction, 28–32. *See also* timber
framing
frost heaving, dealing with, 51

G

gates, 110–25
braces, 113–15
building, 120–23
closers, 120
design options, 124–25
gateposts, 115–17
hardware for, 117–20
hinges, 118
latches, 119–20
planning, 113–20
types of, 112
gazebos, 148–67
building a Victorian, 153–65
design of, 150–53, 166–67
finishing up, 164–65
the floor, 156–59
framing, 159–61
posts, layout for and setting, 155–57, 168
the roof, 159, 161–64

J

joints
butt, 29
fasteners and, 28
lap, 30–31
miter, 32
notches, 29–30, 31
types of, 28

L

layout
of an arch, 131
of border edges, 49
of pole structures, 33–34
of posts for a gazebo, 155
of posts for a pergola, 128
stick, using a, 103
lumber. *See* wood

M

materials, bill of, 174–75

P

paint, 25–26. *See also* finishes
parallel-strand lumber (PSL), 181
pergolas
posts, layout of, 128
with seats, building, 139–41
siting, 141
See also arbors, pergolas, and trellises
planning structures, 168–75
building permits and variances, 173–74
estimating and ordering materials, 174–75
finding inspiration, 169–71
photo mockups, 169–70
working drawings, 170–72
pole construction, 32–40
backfilling, 37–40
digging post holes, 35–37
layout, 33–34
placing posts, 37
posts
depth of holes for, 35
digging holes for, 35–37
for gates, 115–17
installing and trimming for fences, 100–103
layout of, 128
leveling holes for, 132–33
shaping caps for fence, 102
pressure-treated lumber, 18, 19, 22, 79, 179–83

R

railroad ties, 183
raised beds, 76–89
designing, 78–79, 88–89
filling, 87
freestanding lumber beds, building, 83–84
layout and preparation, 79–80